Fabricating Faith

Fabricating Faith

How Christianity Became a Religion
Jesus Would Have Rejected

Richard Hagenston

POLEBRIDGE PRESS

Salem, Oregon

Cover and interior design by Robaire Ream

Library of Congress Cataloging-in-Publication Data
Hagenston, Richard, 1943-
  Fabricating faith : how Christianity became a religion Jesus would have rejected / Richard Hagenston.
     pages cm
  Includes bibliographical references.
  ISBN 978-1-59815-146-6 (alk. paper)
  1. Christianity--Miscellanea. I. Title.
  BR124.H34 2014
  230--dc23
                                                                    2014015231

In grateful memory of Ernest and Carrie, my parents

Contents

Abbreviations

1,2 Cor	1,2 Corinthians
1,2 Kgs	1,2 Kings
1,2 Sam	1,2 Samuel
1,2 Thess	1,2 Thessalonians
Dan	Daniel
Deut	Deuteronomy
Exod	Exodus
Ezek	Ezekiel
Gal	Galatians
Gen	Genesis
Hos	Hosea
Isa	Isaiah
Jer	Jeremiah
Lev	Leviticus
Matt	Matthew
Mic	Micah
Num	Numbers
Phil	Philippians
Ps(s)	Psalm(s)
Rom	Romans
Zech	Zechariah

A Most Unlikely Religion

This book is about solving a deep mystery of Christianity's origins, one that begins with the great irony that Christianity is a religion largely of Gentiles who literally worship Jesus, for Jesus' attitude toward Gentiles was mostly one of disgust. My professors at Wesley Theological Seminary only hinted at that and then left it alone, lest the implications become too troublesome. But there is no denying that the gospels show that Jesus disliked most Gentiles and said that what he offered was not for them.

Some of my earliest memories are the words of a song: "Jesus loves me! This I know, for the Bible tells me so." Since early childhood I found comfort in that. I would still like to think that when Jesus urged his followers to love others as they loved themselves, he would have included Gentiles like me as among those to be loved. But although that is who I want Jesus to be, the gospels offer little assurance on that. To the contrary, Jesus had such a hard edge when it came to Gentiles that he had his own unflattering term for them—dogs.

Jesus made his unfavorable opinion of Gentiles clear on many levels. He said that what he was offering was strictly limited to Jews, sending his apostles out with firm instructions to "go nowhere among the Gentiles" (Matt 10:5). Or as he put it in Matt 15:24, "I was sent only to the lost sheep of the house of Israel." He also used the Gentiles as examples of what not to do. For example, in the Gospel of Matthew Jesus introduces the Lord's Prayer by telling his followers not to "heap up empty phrases as the Gentiles do" (Matt 6:7).

It is true that in Chapter 8 of Matthew and Chapter 7 of Luke the Bible records Jesus as healing a servant of a Roman soldier. Both gospels mention as reasons not just the soldier's faith but also his admission that he was unworthy of Jesus' attention. Perhaps Jesus assumed the servant was a Jew, because when he was asked to heal someone who was indisputably a Gentile, he said no. A Gentile woman asked for healing for her daughter, and Jesus' first response was to totally ignore her. Knowing his attitude, his disciples urged him to silence her pleas not by helping her but by sending her away. Even when she knelt before him, he bluntly refused to help, saying that children's food can't be given to dogs (Matt 15:21–28). The healing came, but only after the woman admitted that as a Gentile she was a dog and pointed out that even dogs eat scraps from their masters' table.

Further confirmation that Jesus had a very harsh attitude toward Gentiles comes from the fact that even as they sought to make converts, his disciples perpetuated a similar attitude after Jesus died. People who were not circumcised and did not live like Jews were not welcome. This drew Paul into trouble when he opened the Jesus fellowship to Gentiles. In fact, Paul writes that those who had resisted him on this included Cephas, also known as none other than the Apostle Peter, and men sent by Jesus' brother James (see Gal 2:11–14).

And yet within a few decades after Jesus' condemnation by the high priest and some others, followed by his execution by the Romans, many Gentiles already regarded Jesus as their savior who had died on the cross to pay the penalty for their sins. This concept of salvation through blood sacrifice, however, not only ignored what Jesus actually taught about forgiveness but could not have been in greater contradiction with it. As we will see, it was so against his teachings that it would likely have horrified him as slander against the Eternal.

To add to the irony, the contrast with who and what Jesus himself said he was expanded until he began to be worshiped as a deity, totally ignoring what he said was the most important tenet of his faith.

Measured by the teachings of the man for whom it is named, Christianity is indeed a most unlikely religion. How could it have arisen in apparent contradiction of Jesus' own words? In this book we will examine this mystery. In so doing we will see how Christianity has presented the death of Jesus as a sin offering only by drawing on a disputed and self-serving plan crafted centuries before the birth of Jesus by some brutal, power-hungry priests. And we will see how

Christianity effectively built its status and fortunes only by ignoring much of what Jesus taught. Finally, we will consider some options for what this might mean for today, including perhaps the possibility that the true good news of the gospel is one of reconciliation with God and neighbor that is even more profound than many Christians have realized.

The Challenge of Understanding the Bible

To begin to understand how Christianity arose in spite of some key teachings of Jesus, we need to consider some of the special difficulties in understanding the Bible. Many people would say there are no problems here—one simply reads and accepts. However, taking the Bible seriously for all it says is not that simple. Finding one's own understanding of the Bible invariably involves creating biblical topiary. I used to live near the Ladew Topiary Gardens in Maryland where remarkable objects are sculpted out of shrubbery, including a fox hunt with dogs, horse and rider leaping a fence, and, of course, the fox. Although creating topiary is a complex art, it ultimately comes down to pruning away what is not wanted to leave only the desired object. And that is what people often do when they read the Bible. They select just what they want. But unlike topiary gardeners with their shears, practitioners of biblical topiary are often oblivious to what they are leaving out. And some of them become extremely hostile to anyone who calls their attention to parts of the Bible that they are ignoring to make its message fit their beliefs.

Serious study of the entire Bible, and not just the parts with which we are comfortable, requires accepting the fact that much of the Bible does not make sense. Part of the problem is that a vast number of verses in the Hebrew Bible cannot be translated from the Hebrew text with certainty. Bible translators have typically withheld from their readers the fact that their work includes a huge number of guesses, often based on the guesses of those who came before them, which may or may not match the original intent. What many Christians believe to be the perfect Word of God is thus in many Bible verses an uncertain effort to keep the text flowing smoothly over stumbling places that are unclear in Hebrew because of ancient copying errors or words otherwise not understood. And any thought that God is inspiring the translators to produce the correct meaning faces the problem that, if so, he would often seem to be inspiring different translators to make different guesses.

Some modern Bible translations do note that the meaning of certain passages is unclear. Very up-front about this issue is the English translation of the Hebrew Bible published in 1985 by the Jewish Publication Society. The JPS translation of what Jews call the Tanakh, a term based on abbreviations of the section names by which Jews organize the same books that Christians call the Old Testament, has hundreds of pages with footnotes pointing out something on the page that is uncertain. Not just a few, but hundreds. And even that translation continues the practice of inserting the translators' guesses. If Bible translators were to be totally forthright about the matter, their work would be riddled with gaps or even diversions into nonsense, insights into reality that many readers would find unsettling.

Even when the text's meaning is clear, both the Hebrew Bible and New Testament have many portions that don't make sense because of contradictions. As one of many examples that could be given, let's look at Chapter 33 of Exodus. Verse 11 says that God spoke to Moses face to face as if to a friend. But Verse 20 has God telling Moses that he cannot see his face because no person can see his face and live. All we can say about these verses is that there were two traditions about this and that Exodus gives both of them. However, taken together those verses make no sense at all. Furthermore, there is no way to resolve the matter.

Sometimes there are ways to resolve differences that lead to contradictions. Occasionally this is because of what is known apart from the Bible about the history of those times. Sometimes it comes down to a matter of precedence—which of two traditions clearly came first. Sometimes there is another part of the Bible that presents what is in effect a tiebreaker. And sometimes it is a combination of these. It's a process that out of necessity we must use as we explore the matter before us. To look at the process, let's use the part of the New Testament that is probably best known to most people, the story of the birth of Jesus.

As the story goes, Jesus' mother, Mary, was a virgin who became pregnant by the Holy Spirit. She and her husband, Joseph, lived in Nazareth. However, as the time approached for her to deliver there was a census that required everyone to go to their own hometown to be counted for the purpose of taxation. Since Joseph was a descendant of King David, they went to David's hometown of Bethlehem.

In Bethlehem there was no room in the inn, so Jesus was born in a stable with a manger for a crib. At about this time three wise men from the East arrived in Jerusalem asking where they could find the child born to be king of the Jews, for while in the East they had seen his star and had come to worship him. Hearing about this King Herod asked his advisers where the messiah would be born. After learning that the scriptures said Bethlehem, Herod called in the wise men and told them to go to Bethlehem. And then Herod asked the wise men to report to him as soon as they found the child, so he could worship him too.

After the wise men left Herod the star they had been following went ahead of them and stopped over the stable where the child was. There they knelt and worshiped him and gave him gifts. Then, warned in a dream not to return to Herod, they went home by another road. Furious that the wise men did not tell him where to find the child, Herod ordered the slaughter of all boys two years of age and younger living in or near Bethlehem.

After the wise men left, an angel warned Joseph in a dream to take his family to Egypt because Herod was seeking to kill the child. After Herod's death an angel, again in a dream, told Joseph that it was safe to return home, and so the family returned to Nazareth.

And thus we have the nativity story. Or maybe not.

First, we need to understand that having Jesus born in Bethlehem was essential for both Matthew and Luke because scripture predicted that a new ruler of Israel would come from there (see Mic 5:2 and the quotation of it in Matt 2:5–6). However, only the Gospel of Luke says that Jesus' parents traveled from Nazareth to Bethlehem to be enrolled in a census. The Gospel of Matthew mentions nothing about that journey or the census, because in Matthew Jesus' parents already lived in Bethlehem. Only Luke says Jesus' parents arrived from Nazareth to find no room in the inn. And none of the gospels say Jesus was born in a stable. That has been assumed from Luke's statement that Jesus was laid in a manger, a feed trough for animals. Matthew never mentions a manger because in that gospel baby Jesus was in a house, presumably the Bethlehem home of his parents.

Also, the Bible never says there were three wise men, only that there were three gifts. And it does not say they went to pay honor to Jesus at the manger. Instead, since the wise men are mentioned only in Matthew, it says they went to the house to find Jesus. People who create nativity scenes with the wise men at the manger have taken it upon themselves to invent a new gospel of their own. Maybe they are thinking of shepherds who appear only in Luke.

As for the census, the author of Matthew probably didn't mention it because he knew it didn't take place at that time. Luke identifies the census as the one when Quirinius was governor of Syria. That's the same census mentioned in Acts 5:37. Quirinius did not arrive in the area until the year 6 CE and ordered the census only at that time. If Jesus was born while Herod the Great was king, Jesus would have been at least ten years old by the time of the Quirinius census.

Some people have tried to make the Gospel of Luke fit reality by claiming that Quirinius must have also been governor earlier and conducted a census as stated in Luke. However, there is no historical basis for this. In the last years of Herod's reign Quirinius was stationed in what is present day Turkey. Also, there was no need for the Romans to conduct a taxation census while Herod or his son and successor Archelaus were in power. Taxation would have been that client kingdom's responsibility. It was only after the Romans deposed Archelaus after ten years of rule following his father's death in 4 BCE that they had a need to find out how many people lived in that region. And, in contrast to Luke's gospel, they didn't make people move to a city of their forefathers to be counted. Instead, just as with censuses taken in our time, they wanted to know who actually lived where. It's astonishing that some people read what Luke says about the census and don't question it by thinking of the chaos that would happen in our day if every census required us to go back to the town of an ancestor.

The author of the Gospel of Luke is presumed to have also written the book of Acts. If so, he clearly knew when the Quirinius census actually took place because he got it right in Acts. In his gospel Luke seems less concerned about historical reality than finding a reason for Jesus to be born in Bethlehem, the town where David was born. Luke's statement that the census required Mary and Joseph to go to the birthplace of David seems especially arbitrary because David lived about a thousand years earlier. Under rules like that I, for one, would have to go to Norway to be counted. What about the many intervening generations of ancestors? In fact, in carrying out a census the Romans cared not at all about people's ancestors. But Luke was so determined to show Jesus as a descendant of David born in the same town that David was that he tried to make the pieces fit the prophecy in the book of Micah even when they did not.

So does that mean that the Gospel of Matthew presents a more reliable picture? Not really.

There is one part of the Matthew story that lends itself to historical verification, and that is the slaughter of male children that Matthew says Herod ordered. In Matthew that threat causes the parents of Jesus to flee with him to Egypt until Herod dies.

As we have seen, the Gospel of Matthew says that the family of Jesus originally had a house in Bethlehem. But Matthew says that after Herod's death they did not return from Egypt to their previous home in Bethlehem of Judea but went on to Galilee to find a new home in Nazareth (Matt 2:21–23):

> Then Joseph got up, took the child and his mother, and went
> to the land of Israel. But when he heard that Archelaus was
> ruling over Judea in place of his father Herod, he was afraid to
> go there. And after being warned in a dream, he went away to
> the district of Galilee. There he made his home in a town called
> Nazareth, so that what had been spoken through the prophets
> might be fulfilled, "He will be called a Nazorean."

Nothing in the Hebew Bible matches the prophecy that is mentioned about being called a Nazorean, so it is uncertain what the author of the Gospel of Matthew might have been referring to. Nonetheless, Matthew has thus made a necessary transition from what that gospel says was an original home in David's birthplace of Bethlehem to Nazareth, which was known as the actual hometown of Jesus.

However, the story about the killing of male children doesn't match what is known about those times, and the fact that it doesn't puts in doubt any involvement by Herod, and with it, the visit by the wise men. Herod was a brutal man who had even his own wife killed, but the historical records of his reign are so detailed that anything as dramatic as a slaughter of innocents would likely have been recorded. That it never happened is further verified by the fact that the author of the Gospel of Luke seems to have never heard of it. In Luke's gospel Mary and Joseph, with nothing to fear, take Jesus to Herod's capital city of Jerusalem where the Temple was for the ritual appropriate for the birth of a child (Luke 2:22–24). Then they immediately return to their home in Nazareth (Luke 2:39). No threat, no massacre, and no trip to Egypt.

More evidence that much of Matthew's story has no historical basis comes from nature itself. Matthew says that the wise men found the child because a star came to rest above him. Go outside some clear night and try to decide which star is directly above you. Without precise measuring instruments it is impossible. People over a range of many miles could conceivably select the same star. Also, stars don't stop in the sky to come to rest over a specific place. In only an hour a star you thought was directly above you will be over a place hundred of miles westward in another time zone because of the rotation of the earth. When difficulties like this are pointed out, some people say that what Matthew describes was something other than an ordinary star, such as an unusual conjunction of bright planets. But that doesn't change the fact that there are no astronomical objects that behave like the star in Matthew's story—not stars, not planets, not comets, nothing.

So why would Matthew wish to create his story? He seems especially interested in matching his version with scripture. The supposed slaughter of children has its prototype in the command by Pharaoh in the first chapter of Exodus to kill all newborn Hebrew males. Just as in Exodus where baby Moses survives to lead his people, Matthew presents baby Jesus as a new Moses who survives to lead his.

Becoming more specific, Matt 2:17–18 says that the killing of boys in Bethlehem was to fulfill Jer 31:15:

> Thus says the LORD: A voice is heard in Ramah, lamentation and bitter weeping. Rachel is weeping for her children; she refuses to be comforted for her children, because they are no more.

And Matt 2:14–15 says that the supposed return of Jesus and his parents from Egypt after Herod's death was to fulfill Hos 11:1b:

Out of Egypt I called my son.

These biblical citations did not make much of an impression on Jews who were familiar with their scriptures. They would have recognized the Jeremiah quotation as referring to conquests by Assyria and Babylonia centuries earlier, which we will look at in the next chapter. And they would have known that the quote from Hosea was understood to refer to calling Israel as a people, not a single individual, out of Egypt during the Exodus. But those words did make a powerful impression on Gentiles who did not have the knowledge of those scriptures to realize the problems with Matthew's references.

When we look at the discrepancies between Matthew and Luke, and consider what is known about that time concerning the census and Herod the Great, we are left with only three consistent details. All of them are names—Jesus, Mary, and Joseph. Nothing else is certain, not even the town that Jesus was born in. Since we know Jesus came from Nazareth, Luke may be correct in saying that his parents lived there before his birth. However, since the Quirinius census didn't take place until ten years after the death of Herod the Great, and because when the census happened people were counted where they lived, there would have been no reason for Mary and Joseph to travel to Bethlehem. That is, if Nazareth had even been part of the Quirinius census, and it was not. Contrary to Luke 2:1, which says that at that time Emperor Augustus issued a decree "that all the world should be registered," when the Quirinius census did happen it included Judea where Bethlehem is but not Galilee where Nazareth is. At that time Galilee was under the reign of another of Herod the Great's sons, Antipas, and Quirinius had no authority over it.

We might expect some guidance on these discrepancies from the Gospel of Mark. Many New Testament scholars consider Mark the earliest gospel to be written and one of the major sources for both Matthew and Luke, which parallel it in many ways. However, Mark opens with Jesus as an adult, with his baptism in the Jordan River by John the Baptist. Mark says that it was then that God proclaimed Jesus to be his son. Mark mentions nothing about the birth of Jesus.

Likewise, the Gospel of John also begins the narrative of Jesus' life with John the Baptist and with Jesus as an adult. Since a virgin birth by the action of the Holy Spirit would have been so remarkable, it seems unlikely that Mark and John would not have mentioned it if they believed such a thing happened. However, we have to be cautious when trying to draw conclusions from silence.

To add to the complications, the birth of Jesus to a virgin is said in Matt 1:22–23 to be the fulfillment of prophecy. The relevant verse is Isa 7:14. The Septuagint, a Greek translation of the Hebrew Bible made about two centuries before the birth of Jesus, does use a word in that verse that can mean "virgin." However, the Hebrew text says only that it was a "young woman," and one who was already pregnant when the prophet wrote centuries before the time of Jesus. This difference with Matthew is reflected in some translations of the Hebrew Bible, but not in others whose translators may not wish to conflict with the gospel.

So, what to make of this? Although usually overlooked, in addition to Matthew and Luke the New Testament has a third description of how Jesus came into the world. It comes from a man who wrote well before the gospels were written. He had spoken with Peter and others who knew Jesus and from them had the opportunity to learn everything he could about the uniqueness of the man he was proclaiming. His name was Paul.

Paul begins his letter to the Romans by introducing Jesus as someone born of the flesh as a descendant of David and declared to be the son of God only through his resurrection (Rom 1:3–4). In other words, the earliest record we have, written by a man who had spoken with those who had personally known Jesus and his mother and brothers, says that Jesus came into the world the same way all of the rest of us did. No virgin birth. And since we know that the hometown of Jesus was Nazareth, it seems likely that he was born there as well.

What principles can we learn from all this about reading and understanding the Bible?

First, the gospel writers were not writing biographies of Jesus in the rigorous sense that we think of as a biography today. They included some historical information, but they arranged it to suit their purposes. And especially important to remember is that they added details of their own creation to say what they wanted people to believe about Jesus. There could be no more direct way to present Jesus as the son of God than to say that he was conceived by God. The gospel writers wrote to fulfill their own agendas, and we will be encountering other biblical examples of writing intended to further specific agendas, sometimes contradicting other positions that are also found in the Bible. For many writers of the Bible—and as we will see, the interpreters who gave Christianity its earliest creeds— meeting their personal agendas was paramount.

Also, we see that if there is conflicting information about Jesus and some of it is more favorable to Jesus than the rest, the less favorable is more likely to be accurate. This is because the New Testament writers would have had no reason to create a less favorable story about Jesus than what they understood to have actually happened. Any incentive to change history would have been just the opposite, to create a more favorable view of Jesus. For example, as we have seen, Paul's letter to the Romans conflicts with Matthew and Luke in presenting a much less remarkable version of Jesus' birth. If a virgin birth had taken place, Paul would have heard about it from Peter or others and would surely have mentioned it. Thus, we can conclude that the less remarkable version, Paul's, is more likely to be correct.

And then there is what can be learned from the reaction that some people have to information such as that in this chapter. The differences in what some books of the Bible report about the birth of Jesus should be of no surprise to anyone who has seriously read the New Testament. That these differences are a surprise to many shows that it is possible for some people to be so fixed upon what they want to believe that reading anything different in the Bible fails to register at all. This applies to passages that people latch onto to support their beliefs to the exclusion of other Bible passages that may contradict their personal convictions. If you are of such strongly traditional faith that you are not open to seeing anything in the Bible that you may have overlooked, even words of Jesus, you may not wish to continue with this book.

As stated in the first paragraph of this chapter, there are so many aspects of the Bible that don't fit with one another that finding one's own understanding invariably involves creating biblical topiary— trimming some things away in order to emphasize what we want to keep. Within these pages we will be doing some biblical topiary. It is inevitable. Everyone who seeks to take the Bible seriously does this, whether they realize it or admit it. But in this book we intend to be honest about those parts of the Bible that we are trimming and why we believe they do not accurately reflect the reality of those times.

Now let's look at some historical background that we will need to know as we continue.

Two Concepts of God

Since traditional Christianity assumes that Jesus died for the sins of others, I have long wondered why most Christians don't think to ask where the idea that God's forgiveness requires a bloody death came from. In fact, in the time of Jesus it was just one of two highly conflicting concepts of God. Is God primarily a God of justice, or a God of mercy? How these two ideas evolved and were later understood in the time of Jesus play a major role in understanding the actual teachings of Jesus. And this helps us understand how the church has come to present Jesus as a sacrificial Lamb of God who died for the sins of the world.

To uncover the origins of this tension between mercy and justice, we need to go back to the time when Israel, united as a single kingdom under David and his son Solomon, split in two after Solomon's death. Solomon's taxation policies had caused unrest, especially surrounding perceived favoritism to the southern part of the kingdom and the capital city of Jerusalem. The formal break happened after Solomon's son and successor, Rehoboam, proved to be even harsher than his father was. After the split there was a southern kingdom, Judah, with its capital and religious center in Jerusalem, and a northern kingdom, Israel, with its capital in Shechem and worship centers in Dan and Bethel.

These two kingdoms had much in common, especially a common heritage of the origins of their people. But they also had differences in which each positioned itself as the most authoritative when it came to tradition and religious practice. That common heritage and those differences led to the writing of two significant documents that were likely based on the work of earlier scribes and editors who had drawn on stories that had long been handed down orally.

Today biblical scholars commonly call those two documents J and E for the words that they use for God. J was written in the southern kingdom of Judah and is commonly designated J from its word for God, *Yahweh*, actually the divine name, which begins with the letter J in the German language of scholars who pioneered this source theory. E was written in the northern kingdom of Israel. It gets its designation from its use of the word *Elohim* for God, especially its exclusive use of Elohim prior to God's revelation of his name to Moses in Exodus 3. Today we find J and E interwoven in the early books of the Bible, but they were once separate. And, as we will see, they also came to be interwoven with another document now commonly called P that we will look at in more detail later.

In spite of their similarities concerning the history of the Israelites, J, E, and P differ enough in emphasis, style, and vocabulary that scholars have been able to identify which passages of the Bible likely originally belonged to each. This work dates back more than two centuries and has followed a path that sometimes reads like a detective story. The work goes on, but many biblical scholars are in general agreement about the broad framework. Concerning the identity of these documents and their significance, in this chapter I will largely be guided by the presentation of Richard Elliott Friedman in his book *Who Wrote the Bible?*[1]

The two kingdoms of Israel and Judah coexisted for two centuries. Then in the year 722 BCE Assyria conquered the northern kingdom and it disappeared forever. Many of its people were led off to exile, but others were able to go south to safety in Judah.

With the people who fled from the north to Judah to escape the Assyrians came E, and that posed a problem. There was now just one kingdom but two histories, both E and J, similar in many ways, but with significant differences of special importance to the peoples of each original kingdom in which those documents were written. Because of their differences, keeping both of them could prove awkward. However, to keep one and discard the other could cause considerable dissent among many of the people then living in Judah. In an attempt to resolve the matter, they were woven together with some skilled and diplomatic editing into a document that biblical scholars now commonly call JE.[2]

The consolidation of documents—J with E, and later with P—led to doublets that can be found in the early books of the Hebrew Bible. When J and E offered slightly different versions of the same event, often both were kept or combined. In some cases a portion of each was used to craft a single story. Friedman provides multiple examples. To cite one, the "theophany of Moses," a direct encounter of Moses with God, begins with a portion of E (Exod 33:12–23) and then continues with a portion of J (Exod 34:1–10).

Sometimes we see clearly contradictory versions of the same event. For instance, J from the southern kingdom has the northern kingdom's capital of Shechem obtained through treacherous deceit followed by a massacre (Genesis 34). The authors of E in the northern kingdom could not accept that. Instead, they wrote that land in Shechem was honorably obtained through a purchase (Gen 33:18–19).

Some people are uncomfortable with the thought that the Bible was assembled over time from a variety of sources, let alone sources that sometimes competed with one another. Dramatic differences such as those about how Shechem was obtained make clear that there actually once were separate stories. As for Shechem, those who combined J and E included both versions. For them, creating an anthology that honored both traditions was more important than eliminating contradictions.

One thing both J and E agreed upon, and that carried over into the combined JE, was an understanding of God as merciful and forgiving.[3] One of the most significant expressions of this is in Exod 34:6–7a in which God passes before Moses and proclaims himself as being, "The LORD, the LORD, a God merciful and gracious, slow to anger, and abounding in steadfast love and faithfulness, keeping steadfast love for the thousandth generation, forgiving iniquity and transgression and sin."

But then someone who did not like the idea of a merciful God came along and added words that were in total contradiction, saying that God was "yet by no means clearing the guilty, but visiting the iniquity of the parents upon the children and the children's children, to the third and fourth generation" (Exod 34:7b).

This startling shift in message within a single passage leads us to the fact that some priests in Judah decided they could reap an advantage by challenging JE's understanding of God as merciful. From them came another document, this time presenting God as a God of strict justice requiring blood sacrifice for the forgiveness of sin, and more specifically, sacrifice performed only through them. At least one person in that group decided to make the case on their behalf by writing a competing history. Because it reflects priestly concerns and agendas, that is the document now commonly called P. To begin to understand how P came to be we need to consider the tribe of Levi.

The Levites were not given their own tribal territory. Instead, as the priestly class, they received several cities of their own and the related pastureland scattered throughout the territories of the other tribes.

You might think that any Levite could perform any priestly function, but instead the Levites broke up into clans with competing claims on authority and responsibility. The writing of P reflects the claim by a specific group of priests to continue what had been their monopoly over the Jerusalem Temple. They were Aaronites, meaning that they understood themselves to be descendants of Moses' brother Aaron.

Aaronites had been the high priests at the first Jerusalem Temple ever since its construction by King Solomon. However, the fall of the northern kingdom and the merging of J with E posed a problem that could lead to a challenge to their authority. E was very favorable to Moses. It thus could be seen in support of another group of priests who understood themselves to be Moses' descendents and had been very influential before the time of the monarchy. Even worse for the Aaronites, E was harshly critical of their ancestor Aaron, as exemplified by the notorious episode of the making of an idolatrous golden calf by *Aaron* (Exod 32:1–4).

To enhance Aaron's image, the author of P dealt with the troublesome matter of the golden calf by omitting the entire issue. And he made Aaron largely co-equal with Moses in authority and respect. In P, when something important is being accomplished, it is not just with Moses as leader but with Moses and the priest Aaron (see Num 1:17, 44; Num 3:38–39; and Num 4:34, 37, 41, 45–46). Finally, to cement a lofty image for Aaron, in P God often speaks not just to Moses but to Moses *and* Aaron (see Num 2:1 and Num 4:1, 17).

To support the idea that only the Aaronites could rightfully perform sacrifice, the author of P thoroughly deleted all examples of sacrifice performed before the time of Aaron. In P, for instance, the story of Abraham and Isaac is nowhere to be found. Since Abraham lived before Aaron, Abraham could not be one of Aaron's descendants. To leave in the story of Abraham sacrificing the ram that was provided in place of his son Isaac would result in showing a non-Aaronite making a valid sacrifice. That is something the author of P could not condone, although it meant ignoring an important part of his people's traditions.

In P there are no sacrifices until the consecration of Aaron and his sons as priests that we find toward the end of the book of Exodus. Then the book of Leviticus begins by specifically declaring that it was Aaron's descendants rather than anyone else who were to be the priests in charge of sacrifices (Lev 1:5–11). This is reinforced in Num 18:1–7, which says that other Levites can serve only as assistants, but not in the holiest areas, and that anyone other than an Aaronite who approaches the altar is to be put to death. Thus the author of P and those he represented played very rough, demanding the killing of challengers.

The early chapters of Leviticus offer great detail on different types of offerings: burnt offerings, grain offerings, offerings of well being, and, beginning with Chapter 4, sin offerings. Initially sin offerings are shown as being only for unintentional sin (Lev 4:2), but later for all types of sin (Lev 16:16). In a stern refutation of the merciful God of JE, the message is clear: The author of P wanted everyone to believe that God won't forgive without first being appeased by a bloody death—not just a sacrificial offering, but a blood sacrifice. And, as we have seen, he insisted that only the priests of his group were authorized to officiate.

The insistence that God's forgiveness could be mediated only through them gave the Aaronites enormous authority over anyone who would accept it. And the author of P also turned this into an opportunity to ensure not just his group's power but also its income. For he wrote that whether an offering was of grain or an animal, the priests were entitled to a portion of each (for examples see Lev 2:1–3 and 7:31–36, and Num 18:8–14). In fact, the Numbers passage says they were to have not just a portion, but the best portion of everything.

This view of sacrifice to satisfy a God of strict justice was not only self-serving for the Aaronite priests but also a huge break with the much older tradition of a God of great love and mercy. To understand how great that break was, realize that JE uses the word *atonement* only once, in reference not to a sacrifice but to an effort by Moses to mediate with God about the idolatrous golden calf made by Aaron (Exod 32:30). Although examples of sacrifice occur in JE, such as Abraham's sacrifice of a ram instead of his son Isaac, sacrifice in JE is never to atone for sin. To repeat, JE has no instance of a sacrifice to atone for sin. Not one. In JE, God is so faithful and merciful that such a thing is not even to be conceived. Instead, in JE sacrifice is always an offering to demonstrate gratitude or faithfulness to God. It is the same concept of a merciful and forgiving God that also occurs elsewhere in the Bible, such as in some of the psalms—but not in P, which never even once has the word "mercy."

The author of P carefully crafted his document as a replacement for JE, with many of the elements of JE, including a creation story. He ignored everything from JE that was not favorable to his cause and added new material to support his own position.

Then, as Friedman points out, something very ironic took place. Instead of letting P stand alone as its author intended, just as J and E were combined to form JE, someone combined JE with P. The result is the first four books of the Bible: Genesis, Exodus, Leviticus, and Numbers. This combining of sources explains the dramatic shift from a God of mercy to a God of judgment that we saw within a single passage in Exodus 34. It's also the reason the Bible begins with two very different creation stories. Genesis begins with the P story. Even a cursory look at it shows that it was never intended to literally depict the creation of the world. For instance, although it says light appeared on the first day, there are no sources of light—sun, moon, or stars—until the fourth day. Meanwhile, the story has plants growing and bearing fruit in what would seem to be total darkness. Instead, the most obvious purpose of the P creation story is to serve a priestly agenda. By depicting God as creating the world in six days and then resting on the seventh, it declares a divine precedent for the Sabbath. Then midway through Gen 2:4 comes the JE creation story (originally from J), which presents creation in a significantly different sequence.

The combination of JE with P is also the reason the story of Noah in Genesis has two interwoven versions that differ in the number of animals brought on the ark. The JE story has God ordering up to seven pairs of each animal (Gen 7:2–3). This allowed some animals to be used for a sacrifice of gratitude after the flood subsided (Gen 8:20). However, since for the author of P a valid sacrifice was impossible before the time of Aaron, he wrote a version that says God ordered that only one pair of each animal was to be taken on the ark (Gen 6:19–20). And to firmly stress that no sacrifice was to be done, his version has God telling Noah in that same passage that these single pairs of animals were to be kept alive. Thus we have in Genesis two conflicting and awkwardly combined stories of Noah and the ark.

The P document also gives the laws found in Leviticus. They include what Jesus called, after the commandment to love God with our whole heart (Deut 6:5), the next greatest commandment: to love our neighbor as we love ourselves (Lev 19:18).

We have not discussed Deuteronomy in detail, but with Genesis, Exodus, Leviticus, and Numbers it completes the Torah, the first five books of the Bible. As you may guess, scholars interested in how the Hebrew Bible came to be written see in Deuteronomy a document that they call D. Deuteronomy seems to have been written in part to protest against P, since it says that all Levites can perform priestly functions with no distinction as to who is most important (Deut 18:5–7). And, as do J and E, D views God as primarily a God of mercy rather than a God of justice (Deut 4:31):

> Because the LORD your God is a merciful God, he will neither
> abandon you nor destroy you; he will not forget the covenant
> with your ancestors that he swore to them.

Also, although Deuteronomy gives rules for sacrifice, there is no mention at all of a sacrifice for sin. Instead, all sacrifices are in the nature of donations and tithes in grateful response to blessings received.

From the standpoint of our inquiry in this book, the point is that Jews of the first century CE could choose from their scripture and traditions two very different understandings of how to obtain God's forgiveness. Some took the position of P and viewed God as a God of strict justice for whom blood sacrifice is essential. But even in Old Testament times there were those who disputed that position in favor of the far older tradition of a God of mercy. For an example in the Hebrew Bible of the tension between these two views, we can look at Psalm 51. That psalm was written during the Babylonian exile, considered in more detail in the next chapter. It was a time when Temple sacrifice was impossible because of the destruction of the original Temple. To offer comfort in this situation, the psalmist climaxes a plea for God's forgiveness and salvation by proclaiming a God of mercy for whom sacrifice is not only not required but not even wanted (Ps 51:16–17):

> For you have no delight in sacrifice; if I were to give a burnt offering, you would not be pleased. The sacrifice acceptable to God is a broken spirit; a broken and contrite heart, O God, you will not despise.

For those in the first century CE who felt the same way, it became understood that all this merciful God requires to forgive is sincere repentance. However, the psalm concludes with a contradictory addition by what was likely a later writer who still believed in the necessity of sacrifice. And this opposite view, that of the importance of sacrifice, was also held by many during the time of Jesus (Ps 51:18–19):

> Do good to Zion in your good pleasure; rebuild the walls of Jerusalem, then you will delight in right sacrifices, in burnt offerings and whole burnt offerings; then bulls will be offered on your altar.

As we will later see, an important key to the matter addressed in this book is which New Testament figures saw God as merciful, requiring only a contrite heart, and which accepted the priestly agenda of a God of strict justice who demands a bloody death before he will forgive.

The Hope for a Messiah

The next aspect of Judaism in the first century CE that we need to consider concerns the hope for a messiah held by many Jews of that time. For that we begin with their bewilderment about the end of a royal line of David whose reign was supposed to continue forever.

According to 2 Samuel, God declared to the prophet Nathan that David and his offspring would always rule Israel. In 2 Sam 7:16 Nathan proclaims this to David as the word of God:

> Your house and your kingdom shall be made sure forever before me; your throne shall be established forever.

That did not mean that the Davidic king would always find unqualified favor with God. David himself was a flawed man who arranged to have the husband of Bathsheba killed in battle so he could cover up his adultery with her and have her for himself. And the northern part of what had been David's kingdom broke away because of the shortcomings of David's son Solomon and Solomon's son and successor, Rehoboam. But the promise made through Nathan was that a king from the line of David would always rule in Jerusalem.

Since the promise of an everlasting Davidic kingship was seen to have come from God himself, a break in that royal line was unthinkable. And yet, just as the northern kingdom was conquered by Assyria in the year 722 BCE, the southern kingdom—including Jerusalem—was eventually conquered by the Babylonians. Many of its leading citizens were exiled to Babylonia, including the king, Jehoiachin. Another from the line of David, Jehoiachin's uncle Zedekiah, was then placed on the throne as a Babylonian vassal. After about nine years he rebelled against the Babylonian king, Nebuchadnezzar. The response, in the year 587 BCE, was truly dreadful. Thousands of additional Jews were exiled to Babylonia. Zedekiah was forced to watch as his sons were executed before him, and then he was blinded and carried to Babylon in chains. Jerusalem was destroyed, including the Temple. Thus the rule of kings from the line of David ended.

In 538 BCE the Persians conquered Babylonia. The Persian emperor, Cyrus the Great, allowed those Jews who wished to do so to return to Jerusalem and build a new Temple. To offer encouragement during the exile, Ezekiel had prophesied that it would end with a restoration that included a Davidic kingship that would last forever (see Ezek 37:24–26). Although the return was led by Zerubbabel, a grandson of Jehoiachin, he served only as governor on behalf of the Persians, not as king. The Second Temple was dedicated on Passover in 516 BCE, but there was no return of the Davidic kingship under the Persians, or under the Greeks following Alexander the Great's defeat of the Persians in 331 BCE, or under the Romans that were in power during the time of Jesus.

Between the Greeks and the Romans there was a brief interlude, a return to Jewish rule. From the events that led to it came a hope that was to offer a powerful fascination for many Jews of the first century CE, the idea that a new age of righteousness was coming with the restoration of the Davidic kingship. For how that idea came to be, we need to look at two books, one that is in the Bible and one that is not.

The biblical book is Daniel. Although it is set during the time of the Babylonian exile, it is probably the last book of the Hebrew Bible to be written. The first six chapters relate stories about the character Daniel, such as the story of him in the lion's den, his interpretation of King Nebuchadnezzar's dreams, and the story of the writing on the wall. Chapters 7–12 are an apocalypse, a type of literature well known to Jews of the first century CE and well known to Christians today, since the last book of the New Testament, Revelation, is an apocalypse.

A typical characteristic of apocalyptic literature is that it purports to be written in an earlier time than it actually was and seeks to establish its credibility by claiming to predict events that had actually already taken place. It then goes on to address issues of the author's own day, all the while using strange symbolic language such as beasts to represent characters and events in a kind of code that the people of the time in which the work was actually written would understand. Finally, apocalypses climax in a prediction of the end of the current age and the beginning of a new age in which only God's will prevails.

The apocalypse of Daniel was prompted by some actions of Antiochus IV Epiphanes, a ruler of the Seleucid Empire, one of the successor states to the reign of Alexander the Great after the division of his empire following his death. Antiochus outlawed the Jewish religion in order to impose Hellenistic religious practices and had a statue of Zeus set up on the Temple Mount, something many Jews considered an especially unacceptable abomination. These actions led to a Jewish revolt that was to prove successful in 165 BCE, described in 1 and 2 Maccabees, books that can be found in any Bible that includes the Apocrypha. Today that victory is celebrated each year in the Jewish festival of Hanukkah. Two decades after that military success, a Jewish ruling dynasty was in place, the Hasmoneans. But they were not descendants of David. Also, they had many shortcomings of their own, including taking over the profitable high priesthood for themselves. This ended forever the practice of placing not just an Aaronite in the role of high priest, but a person from a specific line of Aaronites—that of Zadok, who was descended from Aaron's son Eleazer.

Although a vassal of Rome from 63 BCE onward, a Hasmonean kingship remained until 37 BCE when Herod the Great was put in place as the leader of a Roman client state. To aid in the transition he married a Hasmonean princess. But the promise of a Davidic kingship remained unfulfilled, and that brings us back to the book of Daniel. Many Jews of the first century CE found hope in a passage from that book (Dan 7:13–14):

> As I watched in the night visions, I saw one like a human being coming with the clouds of heaven And he came to the Ancient One and was presented before him. To him was given dominion and glory and kingship, that all peoples, nations, and languages should serve him. His dominion is an everlasting dominion that shall not pass away, and his kingship is one that shall never be destroyed.

The term "human being" in that passage was commonly rendered in Aramaic, the language that Jesus spoke, as "son of man," and that is the way some Bible translations, including the King James Version and the much more recent New International Version, render it. Later portions of Daniel make clear that this son of man was originally thought of not as an individual but as the people of Israel as a whole. But by the first century CE there were those who had come to think of the promised son of man as one person who would be sent by God to throw out the Romans and gather together under a single dominion all the peoples of the world in a just kingdom that would last forever. Since the promise of an everlasting kingdom was offered only to David and his descendants, they felt the son of man would have to be from the line of David. They had a term for the person who would do all these things: the anointed one, the messiah.

This hope was reinforced by another book, also an apocalypse, 1 Enoch. Although not in the Bible, it stood on its own as a book very familiar to Jews in the first century CE. The name of the book comes from a claim that it offers a revelation about a coming end of days received by the patriarch Enoch, who is mentioned in Gen 5:21–24. In keeping with that premise, its actual authors wrote anonymously.

1 Enoch was written and compiled in five main sections, perhaps beginning toward the end of the fourth century BCE and continuing into the first century BCE. It is not certain in which language or languages it was originally written. However, we know it was available in Aramaic, the language spoken by Jesus, since several fragments in Aramaic have been found among the Dead Sea Scrolls. Fragments have been found elsewhere in Greek and Latin, indicating that it was respected enough to have a wide circulation. We know the complete text only because it exists in Ge'ez, also sometimes called Ethiopic, an ancient language of Ethiopia that is still used in the liturgy of some Ethiopian churches.

Most Jews and Christians have not included 1 Enoch in their Bibles. One likely reason is that it was completed too late for Jews to consider it venerable enough for their canon. Even so, some Jews of Ethiopian heritage and some Ethiopian Christians do include it in their biblical canons. And it was considered so authoritative that it is even quoted in the New Testament (Jude 1:14–15).

In 1 Enoch[4] the son of man is introduced in 46:1–5:

And there I saw One who had a head of days,
And His head was white like wool,
And with Him was another being whose countenance had the
  appearance of a man,
And his face was full of graciousness, like one of the holy angels.
And I asked the angel who went with me and showed me all the
  hidden things, concerning that Son of Man, who he was, and
  whence he was, (and) why he went with the Head of Days?
  And he answered and said unto me:
This is the Son of Man who hath righteousness,
With whom dwelleth righteousness,
And who revealeth all the treasures of that which is hidden,
Because the Lord of Spirits hath chosen him,
And whose lot hath the preeminence before the Lord of Spirits
  in uprightness for ever.
And this Son of Man whom thou hast seen
Shall raise up the kings and the mighty from their seats,
And the strong from their thrones.
And shall loosen the reins of the strong,
And break the teeth of the sinners.
And he shall put down the kings from their thrones and kingdoms
Because they do not extol and praise Him,
Nor humbly acknowledge whence the kingdom was bestowed
  upon them.

More details about the son of man are given later in the book,
for example, 48:2–5:

And at that hour that Son of Man was named in the presence
  of the Lord of Spirits,
And his name before the Head of Days.
Yea, before the sun and the signs were created,
Before the stars of the heaven were made,
His name was named before the Lord of Spirits.
He shall be a staff to the righteous whereon to stay themselves
  and not fall,
And he shall be the light of the Gentiles,
And the hope of those who are troubled of heart.

> All who dwell on earth shall fall down and worship before him,
> And will praise and bless and celebrate with song the Lord of
>   Spirits.

With imagery that we will see Jesus applying to himself, the son of man is to sit on a throne of glory (69:27):

> And he sat on the throne of his glory,
> And the sum of judgement was given unto the Son of Man,
> And he caused the sinners to pass away and be destroyed from
>   off the face of the earth,
> And those who have led the world astray.

The influence of 1 Enoch extended beyond giving a general hope to some Jews that God would one day intervene to restore for them a kingdom of righteousness. Portions of the New Testament indicate that 1 Enoch and the book of Daniel had led many in the time of Jesus to believe in an imminent end of the age. And, as we will see, it also had a strong influence on Jesus' understanding of himself.

The Religious Diversity of First-Century Palestine

The remaining background that we need to consider about Jews in the first century CE is that they lived in a time of religious diversity.

To casually lump all Jews together as The Jews, whether in Jesus' time or our own, makes no more sense than referring to The Christians without regard to the wide diversity of religious and political convictions that Christians hold. Also, we need to recognize that in the time of Jesus most Jews did not live in the Jewish homeland but elsewhere in what is called the Diaspora. Among them were descendants of those who never returned from the Babylonian exile, as well as Jews in communities widely scattered throughout much of the Mediterranean.

As for the religious diversity in first-century Palestine, there were four main Jewish sects, each with its own distinguishing beliefs: the Zealots, the Essenes, the Sadducees, and the Pharisees. Most Jews of the time did not belong to any of these groups, but we still need to consider them because of the influence they had.

"Zealot" is a term broadly applied by first-century Jewish historian Josephus to Jewish rebel groups that were more of a political movement than a religious one. They began with dissatisfaction over the Roman tax policies imposed in connection with the census by Quirinius in 6 CE. The only biblical reference to the Zealots is in a listing of the apostles of Jesus, which refers to "Simon who was called the Zealot" (Luke 6:15).

The Zealots represented a contrasting view to the messianic hope that God in his own time would restore for Jews an independent kingdom. They were not willing to wait. The word "zealot" has the same Greek and Latin roots as the word "zeal," but the Zealots' zeal was to have tragic consequences for all Jews.

The extremism of the Zealots led to a revolt against the Romans that began in the year 66 CE. The Zealots have been called the first terrorists because some of them had no problem with killing anyone that they felt was standing in their way—not just the Romans they were trying to overthrow but also Jews they considered not properly supportive of their goals. The resulting factions instigated what amounted to a brutal Jewish civil war. By the time the Romans put down the rebellion, possibly more Jews had died at the hands of other Jews than had been killed by the Romans.

A particularly despised act of the Zealots was burning a large stockpile of dried food that had been gathered in Jerusalem in anticipation of the Roman siege of the city. They apparently felt that with no food all of the city would immediately rally with them for what they hoped would be a quick victory against the Romans, but their act only led to the unnecessary suffering of many.

The Zealots' ruthlessness backfired when the Romans not only put down the rebellion in 70 CE but also destroyed the Temple. Thus Jews lost what had been the primary center of their worship. This was especially unfortunate since it came only a short time after the completion of a decades-long building project begun by Herod the Great to make the Temple one of the most magnificent buildings in the world.

The last stand of the Zealots came at Masada, a fortress built by Herod the Great high on an isolated plateau that the Sicarii, an especially violent extremist splinter group, had conquered and had been using as a base of operations. The Romans entered the fortress only after a huge effort in building a siege ramp. When they finally battered down the fortress wall in 73 CE, they found more than nine hundred inhabitants—men, women, and children—dead. To avoid a religious prohibition against suicide, they had killed one another, all except for the suicide of the last one to take part in the slaughter. Apparently, they did not all die willingly. We know this and what had happened because there were seven survivors, two women and five children who had successfully hidden to escape the carnage. Thus came the end of the Zealots. It is important to remember that in the time of Jesus' ministry there was an underlying tension that only about four decades later was to lead to these events.

The Essenes are not mentioned in the Bible, but some feel that because of his ascetic lifestyle John the Baptist may have been an Essene. Essenes tended to live a communal life characterized by collective ownership, volunteer poverty, abstinence from worldly pleasures, and dedication to peace and service to one another. They had messianic expectations and looked toward an imminent end of the age. As part of their piety, like many other Jews of that period and ours, they engaged in ritual immersion, a subject discussed further in the next chapter. Some believe that the community at Qumran, a site on a dry plateau near the northwestern shore of the Dead Sea, was an Essene settlement. If that is the case, we may owe to them the existence of the Dead Sea Scrolls found in caves at Qumran in 1947. The Essenes disappeared from history after the Roman destruction of the Jerusalem Temple in 70 CE. In fact, Qumran may have been taken by the Romans as early as 68 CE.

That leaves us to consider the two major Jewish sects mentioned in the New Testament, the Sadducees and the Pharisees, and the tensions between them.

The Sadducees were not a group that just anyone could join. They were the elite, the aristocrats. They came from priestly ancestry and as priests were responsible for the maintenance of the Temple. The Sadducees were not only in charge of the Temple, they were dependent on it. Thus they stressed what they saw as the necessity of Temple sacrifice. They also had political responsibilities, including mediating relationships with the Romans. Along with some leading members of the Pharisees, Sadducees served on the Sanhedrin, the Jewish high court whose members met in the Temple.

The Sadducees disagreed with the Pharisees on several points, including the authority of an oral tradition about the Torah—that is, the first five books of the Bible—and whether or not there is an afterlife. We will look in more detail at these matters very shortly.

The Pharisees were the largest Jewish sect in the first century CE. The New Testament says that Jesus harshly criticized the Pharisees as hypocrites. Although some likely were, as with any group, the Pharisees as a whole had a piety that attracted great respect among many Jews of their time. For example, they were unique in insisting on adherence of the Temple purity laws outside the Temple. Their belief that the sacred could exist beyond the Temple led them to treat their home life with the same respect as the Temple itself. And although the Sadducees saw the Temple and its priests as the sole authoritative focus for religious gathering, the Pharisees also placed emphasis for scripture study and teaching on local synagogues.

These were led by teachers learned in the Torah who were respected not because of any priestly status but because of their piety, knowledge, and insight.

In contrast with the Sadducees, who believed that there is no existence after death, the Pharisees believed in a resurrection of the dead, specifically, a physical resurrection of the body. They did not accept the Greek concept of the separation of body and soul, so there was no thought of the soul going off by itself to an otherworldly existence in a heaven somewhere. Jews who accepted the idea of the resurrection saw it as literally a renewed physical life on earth. This had its roots in Ezekiel's vision of the valley of dry bones that had flesh returned to them and were restored to physical life (Ezek 37:13):

> And you shall know that I am the LORD, when I open your
> graves, and bring you up from your graves, O my people.

For Ezekiel this symbolically represented the hope that, after the conquests by Assyria and then by Babylon, Israel would be restored. But it came to be seen as a promise of a personal, earthly resurrection. For example, the last verse of the book of Daniel assumes this in the parting words of the man in Daniel's vision to Daniel (12:13):

> But you, go your way, and rest; you shall rise for your reward at
> the end of the days.

The concept of a physical resurrection may seem strange to our modern minds, but many Christians continue at least to pay lip service to it in the Apostles' Creed that they recite in their worship services. It concludes by affirming belief in "the life everlasting" that follows "the resurrection of the body."

Another major difference between the Pharisees and the Sadducees was the Pharisees' insistence that there was not just one valid expression of Jewish law in the Torah, but two. The Sadducees recognized only the literal written words. The Pharisees, however, recognized both the Written Torah and an Oral Torah, and they believed that the Oral Torah flowed from God with the same authority as the Written Torah. They saw a necessity for an Oral Torah because on many points the Written Torah is rather vague about the specifics. What does it really mean, for example, to keep the

Sabbath? What can a Jew do or not do? It's an issue even today with, for instance, records of some very conservative Jews in Israel stoning ambulances on the Sabbath, while other Jews feel that such acts of mercy are allowed.

The Oral Torah arose from teachings of respected sages that became accepted as authoritative tradition. These rulings were to be eventually gathered into a written work called the Mishnah. It became a basis of the Talmud, a vast work of insights and interpretations that Jews consider, along with the Mishnah, to be sacred. For many Jews the Talmud is studied much more frequently than the Bible itself.

The existence of the Oral Torah explains what may appear to be an inconsistency in the gospels. Jesus said that none of the law could be set aside, and yet there were times when some Pharisees accused him of breaking it. Jesus apparently believed that the vagueness of the Written Torah gave him some interpretive flexibility against the Oral Torah.

And, of course, there were the Gentiles. Although the Sadducees taught that one could become a Jew only by birth, the Pharisees encouraged the conversion of Gentiles. They believed strongly in spreading throughout the world the worship of what they felt was their one true God. With that goal they employed extensive and far-reaching missionary efforts, something that Jesus mentioned not in praise but as part of some harsh criticism (Matt 23:15):

> Woe to you, scribes and Pharisees, hypocrites! For you cross
> sea and land to make a single convert, and you make the new
> convert twice as much a child of hell as yourself.

Jewish missionary outreach ended only when the Roman Empire made Christianity its official religion and ruled that conversion to Judaism was punishable by death.

In the time of Jesus there were, however, Gentiles called God-fearers who had turned away from their pagan practices to worship the one God of Judaism without fully converting. Although they did not submit to circumcision and the Jewish dietary laws, they were welcomed in synagogues. There was even a Court of the Gentiles at the Temple, although they were not allowed into the Temple's more sacred areas.

Gentiles were considered exempt from the obligations of the Torah. The Mishnah states that the Torah applies only to those who are under God's covenant with Israel. Since Gentiles are not under that covenant, the rules and obligations of the Torah do not apply to them. For example, under the purity laws of the Torah, Jewish men are considered ritually unclean after an emission of semen, and Jewish women are considered to be made ritually unclean by their menstrual flow. However, Gentile men and women in the same situations are not considered unclean because they are not under God's covenant with Israel. Just contact with a Jew's semen or menstrual blood would make one unclean, but contact with a Gentile's semen or even menstrual blood would not. In fact, Gentiles—unless they were to formally convert—were discouraged from being circumcised or even attempting to make Temple offerings beyond just paying the Temple tax, because those rituals signified Jewish identity as a people set aside under God's special covenant with Israel.

The one exception to following the same laws as those of Jews was that all peoples, including Gentiles, were considered obligated to follow the so-called Noahide laws. Those were thought of as a binding set of laws for all children of Noah. And since Noah is considered the father of all living people, they were seen as applying to everyone, Jews and Gentiles alike. The Seven Laws of Noah were inferred as follows from Genesis 2 and 9:

- Do not murder.
- Do not steal.
- Do not worship false gods.
- Do not be sexually immoral.
- Do not eat the flesh of an animal that is still alive, considered more broadly to mean do not consume blood.
- Do not curse God.
- Do set up courts of law to bring offenders to justice.

With the Roman conquest and destruction of the Temple in 70 CE, the Sadducees joined the Zealots and Essenes in disappearing from history. They had apparently been too dependent on the Temple to continue without it. There were only two Jewish sects remaining: the Jesus sect that evolved into Christianity, and the Pharisees who preserved the Jewish faith that evolved into the Judaism of today. For reasons we shall see, given the choice, most Jews chose to link their future to the Pharisees and their successors.

And now, with all this background, let's begin to examine how Christianity came to be.

What Jesus Taught about Salvation

In 2009 archaeologists announced the discovery in a Jerusalem excavation tunnel of a mikveh dating back two millennia to the time of the Temple. A mikveh is a pool for Jewish ritual purification. What distinguishes this mikveh is its location, just sixty-five feet from the Western Wall, and its size, as part of a building complex with three halls and with eleven broad steps leading down to the ritual bath. With its nearness to the Temple, it was designed to meet the needs of huge numbers of Jews as they ritually purified themselves before entering the Temple itself.

"Mikveh" is a term unfamiliar to many Christians but represents a facility for ritual immersion that remains essential today. There are several occasions for the required or optional use of a mikveh. One is to mark the transition of a new convert to Judaism. After a convert arises from full immersion under the water they are considered a new person in their relationship to God and the community. In this regard, the comparison of the Jewish mikveh with the Christian baptismal font is inescapable. The most common use of a mikveh is the restoration of ritual purity following a required waiting period after the cessation of a woman's menstrual flow. Some Jewish women of today no longer believe that mikveh immersion is necessary, although others still do.

We have seen in Chapter 3 that in the time of Jesus, Jews had their choice of two views of God—a God of justice who requires sacrifice before he will forgive, and a much older concept of a God of mercy who requires only a contrite heart. For those who believed God requires only repentance to forgive, one use of mikveh immersion was to symbolize the washing away of their sins after they repented.

As for the Temple sacrificial system, its adherents saw it as requiring both sincere repentance and blood sacrifice. By the time of Jesus many of those who believed in the necessity of blood sacrifice, as advanced centuries earlier by the Aaronite priests mentioned in Chapter 3, had moved so far from any understanding of a merciful God that they thought everyone deserved to die for their inevitable sins. Adherents to this point of view believed that, with proper repentance, a sacrificed animal could take the place of the sinner for substitutionary atonement.

The question at hand is which view of forgiveness Jesus took. Did he see God as a God of strict justice requiring sacrifice—especially blood sacrifice—in addition to repentance? Or did he see God as a God of mercy requiring repentance only? To begin to answer that question, we need to look to another mikveh, and to a man named John.

There are specific rules regarding how to build a mikveh and the proper source of its water, but a flowing river such as the Jordan qualifies so long as it is deep enough for complete immersion. As the followers of John the Baptist would have understood, there was nothing unique about what he was doing. He was simply using the Jordan River as a mikveh.

The Bible is very specific about John's purpose. All of the first three gospels say John was offering a baptism of repentance for the forgiveness of sins (Matt 3:11, Mark 1:4, and Luke 3:3). That was forgiveness through *repentance alone*, with no Temple sacrifice. Matthew gives more details confirming that this baptism was for the forgiveness of sins, bypassing the Temple system (Matt 3:5–6):

> Then the people of Jerusalem and all Judea were going out to him, and all the region along the Jordan, and they were baptized by him in the river Jordan, confessing their sins.

Given the choice between a God of justice requiring blood sacrifice before he will forgive and a God of mercy requiring only a contrite heart, John the Baptist clearly proclaimed a God of mercy. The fact that crowds came to him makes obvious that many other Jews of that time had also moved beyond any thought of God requiring the shedding of blood.

This brings us back to the question of what Jesus believed about this matter. Did he believe in a God of justice requiring sacrifice, or a God of mercy requiring only repentance? Since he was a strong supporter of the work of John the Baptist, and was himself baptized by John, Jesus clearly believed in a God of mercy. As we will see, he made this clear by his teachings and the disdain he showed for the Temple system of blood sacrifice.

Both John the Baptist and Jesus had apocalyptic expectations and proclaimed that the end of the age was coming very soon. John said he was offering his baptism of repentance for the forgiveness of sins in preparation for that (Matt 3:2):

"Repent, for the kingdom of heaven has come near."

After John's arrest Jesus continued the same message about the importance of preparing for the new age through repentance alone (Matt 4:17):

From that time Jesus began to proclaim, "Repent, for the kingdom of heaven has come near."

Some comment should be made about the use of the word "heaven" in those last two quotations. We think of heaven as an existence beyond this earth. However, as we will see in the next chapter, the kingdom that was being foreseen was an earthly one, although under the rule of God's anointed one, the messiah. Perhaps Matthew was reflecting Jewish sensitivity about how to refer to God. Even today in contemporary religious commentary by Jews, one sometimes sees "G-d" written instead of "God." In any case, in referring to the kingdom, the other gospels always say "kingdom of God" rather than "kingdom of heaven."

Terminology aside, the point is that for both John and Jesus the way to prepare for the end of the age and the coming of the new one was not to repent and also make a sin offering at the Temple, but only to repent. Before looking more deeply into what Jesus taught about this, it is useful to look at the practices of Jews today concerning repentance, because they give important insight into Jesus' message.

After the destruction of the Temple in 70 CE, Temple sacrifice was no longer possible. Of the Jewish sects during the time of Jesus, the Pharisees alone made a successful transition. They were already using synagogues as meetinghouses and readily expanded their use to prayer and worship. In this process they were able to move away from sacrifice as a necessary addition to repentance. Thus, for them the loss of the Temple was not an unrecoverable disaster. It was their adaptability in finding the sanctity of worship through repentance and prayer that allowed the Pharisees and those who succeeded them to preserve Judaism as a living faith.

Today, as for a great many centuries now, Jews see repentance as the means of atonement. The Jewish calendar has forty days of emphasis on self-examination and repentance, beginning with the thirty-day month of Elul. That leads to the ten High Holy Days, starting with Rosh Hashanah, the Jewish New Year. The period concludes with Yom Kippur, the Day of Atonement, the most sacred day of the Jewish calendar.

The emphasis on repentance during this time is not just repentance to God. Here is some wording for worship during this period from *Gates of Prayer*, a prayer and worship book developed for Reform Jewish congregations. It is in both regular and italic type, to be recited responsively:

> Only for our transgression against God does the Day of
> Atonement atone.
>
> *But for our transgression against another human being it does
> not atone unless we have obtained that person's pardon.*[5]

In other words, Jews believe that God can forgive transgressions against him, but that he cannot routinely give blanket forgiveness for those against people, because he is not the aggrieved party. First, Jews believe, people have to settle those matters with one another. The High Holy Days especially are a time for people to reconcile with one another, and not just with confession and forgiveness, but also by actually seeking to right wrongs that have been done. It is with this preparation of first setting things right in the community that on the Day of Atonement Jews contritely seek God's forgiveness. Also, although repentance and forgiveness are emphasized during this time, no Jew would say that the God of grace and mercy they worship limits the possibility of repentance and forgiveness to just one time of the year.

What does this have to do with Jesus? A great deal, because Jesus drew on the roots of that same tradition. And this puts in perspective a portion of the Lord's Prayer and Jesus' commentary on it (Matt 6:12, 14–15):

And forgive our debts as we have forgiven our debtors. . . . For
if you forgive others their trespasses, your heavenly Father will
also forgive you; but if you do not forgive others, neither will
your Father forgive your trespasses.

The only real difference between these words of Jesus and that
Jewish liturgy is that the liturgy expresses this primarily in terms of
repenting, and Jesus expressed it primarily in terms of forgiving. But
repentance and forgiveness inescapably go together.

The highest obligation that Jesus ever placed on people to get
right with God is to first set things right with other people. That
is so often overlooked that I am going to say it again: *The greatest
requirement that Jesus ever placed on people to obtain their salvation
is to have a contrite heart—not just to God, but first by setting things
right with the other people in their lives.* And Jesus said that someone
who seeks forgiveness must be forgiven, with no grudges allowed
(Luke 17:3–4):

"Be on your guard! If another disciple sins, you must rebuke the
offender, and if there is repentance you must forgive. And if the
same person sins against you seven times a day, and turns back
to you seven times and says, 'I repent,' you must forgive."

It is also important to remember that when Jesus spoke of repentance, he meant not just confronting acts of commission, the
bad things people have done. He also meant confronting and cor-
recting acts of omission, the good things that have been within their
power but that they have neglected to do. In Matthew 25 he stresses
the absolute necessity of outreach such as feeding the hungry, clothing the naked, and caring for the sick and others in need.

The fact that Jesus taught that salvation comes through repentance and reconciliation without blood sacrifice presents a dilemma.
For a key aspect of Christian worship assumes that he was a blood
sacrifice. All of the first three gospels describe the Last Supper,
which is seen as Jesus presenting himself as a sin offering, as in Matt
26:26–28:

While they were eating, Jesus took a loaf of bread, and after
blessing it he broke it, gave it to his disciples, and said, "Take,
eat; this is my body." Then he took a cup, and after giving

thanks he gave it to them, saying, "Drink from it all of you; for this is my blood which is poured out for many for the forgiveness of sins."

What are we to make of the discrepancy? As we saw in Chapter 2, the pieces of the Bible do not always fit together very well, and sometimes we need to make a choice. In this case, do we choose to believe in a God of mercy who was proclaimed by both John the Baptist and Jesus and accepted by a great many people from well before their time to ours? Or do we choose a God of justice who could not forgive the sins of the world unless an innocent person was tortured to death? For now suffice it to say that the description of the Last Supper in the gospels seems to have come after the death of Jesus from someone who was not present at that meal and who believed in a God of justice rather than mercy. Later in this book we will identify who that was, but it is highly unlikely that Jesus himself actually said what is attributed to him at his last meal with his disciples.

To further verify that Jesus believed salvation requires only repentance, unaccompanied by any substitutionary blood atonement, we need only look at the disgust that Jesus expressed toward the Temple system of sacrifice. The gospels (Matt 21:12, Mark 11:15–16, and Luke 19:45) say that Jesus went into the Temple and drove out those who were selling and buying, including the money changers and those who sold doves. In fact, the passage from Mark says that he wouldn't even allow anything to be carried through the Temple. The Gospel of John (2:14–16) expands on this. Although John differs from the other gospels in placing the cleansing of the Temple at the beginning of Jesus' ministry rather than at the end, it says that Jesus felt so strongly about what he considered misuse of the Temple that he used a whip to drive out not only the money changers and sellers of doves but also the sheep and cattle that were there to be sacrificed.

Significantly, Jesus cleansed the Temple of everything that was required for blood sacrifice. For the Temple sacrificial system to be possible, the money changers were essential. Without them people coming from places that used a currency other than that accepted at the Temple and had not brought with them an animal to sacrifice would be unable to buy a dove or whatever else they could afford. Likewise, the sellers were necessary, as were of course the animals to be sacrificed—all of which Jesus drove out.

Jesus certainly would have approved of Temple offerings such as the grain offerings that were traditional for the harvest festival of Shavuot (Pentecost), but they had nothing to do with atonement for sin. Also, as a Jew he would have seen as necessary the ritually proper slaughter of animals for food, such as Passover lambs. However, they too were not offerings for atonement but food prepared under rules that we recognize today as keeping kosher. Furthermore, if a visit to the Temple was impractical, the slaughter of animals for food could be done elsewhere so long as it was done correctly. But as for shedding blood at the Temple with the purpose of seeking God's forgiveness, Jesus' revulsion could not be clearer.

By showing his anger against the practice of blood sacrifice and the system of commerce that supported it, Jesus deeply offended those whose faith told them that God required sacrifice and whose livelihood and position in the community depended on it. The high priest must have seen as a special affront Jesus' position that no priestly mediation was needed to obtain God's forgiveness. Those whom Jesus challenged were so upset that they wanted to kill him, but they dared not at that time because the crowd agreed with Jesus (Mark 11:18).

It has sometimes been argued that the only problem Jesus had with the Temple was corruption, but it clearly goes much deeper than that. When he talked about the proper use of the Temple, he didn't even mention sacrifice. So what did Jesus say the Temple was supposed to be, if not a place for sacrifice? A house of prayer (Matt 21:13, Mark 11:17, and Luke 19:46). In contrast, the P document that we considered in Chapter 3, and from which came the practice of blood sacrifice for sin, never mentions praying to or even praising God. It seems no exaggeration to say that the author of P and those he represented wanted no thought of forgiveness from God that was not mediated through them, for a price. Jesus totally rejected that notion.

Finally, if there was any remaining doubt about the harsh feelings of Jesus toward sacrifice, we have the high regard that he had for Hos 6:6, which says:

For I desire steadfast love and not sacrifice, the knowledge of God rather than burnt offerings.

Jesus refers to that verse from Hosea in Matt 9:13:

"Go and learn what this means, 'I desire mercy, not sacrifice.' For I have come to call not the righteous but sinners."

Jesus refers to it again in a reply to critics who said that his followers were not properly observing the Sabbath (Matt 12:7):

"But if you had known what this means, 'I desire mercy and not sacrifice,' you would not have condemned the guiltless."

Given the fact that Jesus firmly rejected sacrifice and taught that salvation comes solely through repentance, both to one another and to a merciful God, it is inconceivable that he would have ever thought of himself as a sacrificial offering. Since it seems he would have reacted with utter disgust at the thought of being viewed as a sacrificial Lamb of God, this raises the question of how anyone intending to follow him has come to see him that way. We will later explore how that came to be. But now, if Jesus would have disagreed with that, what was his real mission?

What Jesus Said His Mission Was

Just as in the previous chapter we saw John the Baptist at the Jordan River, we begin this chapter with him there as well. As we have seen, there were two parts to his message. One was that he was offering a baptism of repentance for the forgiveness of sins. The other was why he said he was doing it. John the Baptist proclaimed that the end of the age was imminent and that it was crucial for people to promptly set right their relationship with God through repentance to prepare for the new kingdom of God that he was certain was coming very soon.

We saw in the last chapter some gospel verses showing both John the Baptist and Jesus stressing this urgency. In fact all of the first three gospels show Jesus promising that the kingdom of God would arrive within the lifetime of some of his followers (Mark 9:1; also see Matt 16:28 and Luke 9:27):

> And he said to them, "Truly I tell you there are some standing here who will not taste death until they see that the kingdom of God has come with power."

The same point is made elsewhere in only a slightly different way (Matt 24:34, Mark 13:30, and Luke 21:32):

> "Truly I tell you, this generation will not pass away until all these things have taken place."

Jewish expectation was that the kingdom would not be an otherworldly heavenly one, but would definitely be on earth. It was to fulfill the hope that many Jews had of a new age ushered in by one who would gather the nations under the one true God, throw out the Romans, and set up a righteous reign on earth with a restoration of the Davidic kingship. In keeping with this, the examples above confirm that Jesus, too, viewed the kingdom as an earthly one that some people of his time would live to see. Those passages are presented as if events that Jesus said would take place after his resurrection.

However, that seems to have been a context added after the death of Jesus. For those same gospels report words and actions of Jesus before the crucifixion that are clearly those of a man who thought he would live to see the kingdom, too.

How was this to come about? Jesus said he was God's chosen one who was to bring in this new kingdom and rule it. Using a term from both the books of Daniel and 1 Enoch, he saw himself as the apocalyptic son of man and referred to himself numerous times in that way. Here is one example of a clear reference to himself (Matt 8:19–20):

> A scribe then approached and said, "Teacher, I will follow you wherever you go." And Jesus said to him, "Foxes have holes and birds of the air have nests; but the Son of Man has nowhere to lay his head."

Another example is something Jesus said about himself in countering his critics (Matt 11:18–19):

> "For John came neither eating nor drinking, and they say, 'He has a demon'; the Son of Man came eating and drinking, and they say, 'Look, a glutton and a drunkard, a friend of tax collectors and sinners!' Yet wisdom is vindicated by her deeds."

And yet another example (Matt 9:5–6; also see Mark 2:9–11 and Luke 5:23–24):

> "For which is easier to say, 'Your sins are forgiven,' or to say, 'Stand up and walk'? But so that you may know that the Son of Man has authority on earth to forgive sins"—he then said to the paralytic—"Stand up, take your bed and go to your home."

And why did Jesus choose twelve, and exactly twelve, apostles? The gospels offer but one explanation—that it was part of his plan to bring in the kingdom. Reflecting the passage from 1 Enoch that says that the son of man would sit on "the throne of his glory" (69:27), Jesus used the same wording to say that prophecy was to be fulfilled in him. But he also promised his apostles that they would each have their own throne (Matt 19:28):

> Jesus said to them, "Truly I tell you, at the renewal of all things, when the Son of Man is seated on the throne of his glory, you

who have followed me will also sit on twelve thrones, judging the twelve tribes of Israel."

Thus, Jesus said he needed twelve apostles because there were twelve tribes of Israel, even though by this time the original tribal territories were largely irrelevant. This may seem strange to our modern values, but it explains what would otherwise be a mystery—why the apostles argued about who among them was the greatest. The mention of that dispute in Mark 9:33–34 and Luke 9:46 seems odd, since there is no suggestion about the reason for it. But in Luke 22:24–30 we see the context, with the apostles' dispute about greatness and Jesus' promise of thrones for them all linked together in the same passage. That passage has the arguments coming before Jesus' explanation, but the fact that his apostles were already arguing suggests that they already knew of Jesus' plan. The passage indicates that he was mainly asking them to have some humility about it.

Apparently the apostles were not only vying for status but even bragging to their family members about the thrones they expected to receive. Mark 10:35–37 says James and John, the sons of Zebedee, asked Jesus to seat them at his right and left, much to the annoyance of the other apostles. However, in Matt 20:20–21 we see them bringing their mother to make the request. Writing years after the crucifixion, the authors of both Matthew and Mark show Jesus replying with a mention of his impending ordeal. But it seems likely that the roots of those passages actually go back to the time when Jesus was promising an imminent new age with him in charge on his throne, and the apostles on theirs.

How did Jesus plan to bring in the kingdom? The Zealots had hoped for a popular uprising to overthrow the Romans, and perhaps Jesus had hoped for something similar. But in true apocalyptic language he said it would come through the acts of angels under his command, and that the consequences would be brutal for anyone who had not heeded his urgent call to set their lives right through repentance. In his promise of commanding angels, we again have something that may seem mystically strange to our modern minds. However, Jesus was very specific about this in his explanation of the parable of the weeds (Matt 13:36–43):

Then he left that crowd and went into the house. And his disciples approached him, saying, "Explain to us the parable of the weeds of the field." He answered, "The one who sows the good seed is the Son of Man; the field is the world, and the good seed are the children of the kingdom; the weeds are the children of the evil one, and the enemy who sowed them is the devil; the harvest will be at the end of the age. The Son of Man will send his angels and they will collect out of his kingdom all causes of sin and all evildoers, and they will be thrown into the furnace of fire, where there will be weeping and gnashing of teeth. Then the righteous will shine like the sun in the kingdom of their Father. Let anyone with ears listen."

When was all this to begin? When Jesus rode into Jerusalem before Passover, those Jews present who knew their scriptures would have seen him as declaring himself then and there as their king, in fulfillment of these words from Zech 9:9:

Rejoice greatly, O daughter Zion! Shout aloud, O daughter Jerusalem! Lo, your king comes to you; triumphant and victorious is he, humble and riding on a donkey, on a colt, the foal of a donkey.

In Zechariah the words "donkey, on a colt, the foal of a donkey" seem likely to be a poetic literary device to refer to a single animal. Although all three of the other gospels mention only one animal being used that day, Matt 21:7 says that Jesus actually used two as literal fulfillment of Zechariah. Regardless of whether Jesus used one or two animals, he wanted to leave no doubt about the Zechariah reference and the special status as king that he understood himself to have. Furthermore, apart from the reference to Zechariah, there was strong precedent for kingly arrival in a similar way. When Solomon arrived as the king newly appointed by his father, David, he rode on a mule (1 Kgs 1:44).

Lest any doubt remain that Jesus and his followers had an imminent earthly kingdom in mind, Luke says that as he approached Jerusalem there were those who expected Jesus to immediately bring in that new kingdom (Luke 19:11). Jesus did nothing to discourage them from that view. Instead, Luke says that he addressed them with a parable about a man becoming a king. Speaking through t of the main character in the parable, and in words that wer terrible irony because of what would soon happen to him,] poses an utterly horrible end for any opponents (Luke 19:27):

> "But as for these enemies of mine who did not want me to be king over them—bring them here and slaughter them in my presence."

Some have questioned whether the person they imagine Jesus to have been could have actually said that. However, since those words challenge an image of Jesus that even gospel writers were to come to want to project, there would have been no reason to make them up without a tradition that Jesus actually said them.

With his declaration of himself as king, Jesus may very well have felt that events would unfold quickly and that he would soon find himself on that earthly throne of glory of which he had spoken. With such a grand victory in mind, crucifixion would seem an unthinkable possibility. However, although the gospels show that some who welcomed Jesus into Jerusalem indeed saw in him the messianic return of the kingdom of David, there was no popular uprising on his behalf and certainly no support from angels. The divine intervention he expected never came, and without it Jesus found himself in a terrible position. He had infuriated the Jewish high priest and others by condemning Temple practices that had been both a precept of their faith and a source of their power and income. That is a potent combination for offending anyone, and they had already made clear they felt he deserved to die for it. And any Romans who understood the messianic hope would have known that it looked toward the overthrow of the civil authority. Rome tolerated no challenge to its rule.

Jesus' Zech 9:9 claim to kingship was indeed taken seriously, but the result was not Jesus reigning as king. He died on a cross that his executioners sarcastically decorated with the words "King of the Jews." However, before we conclude that this was a failure, we need to look at another possible interpretation.

Overlaid on the message of great urgency in bringing in the kingdom is another theme that seems to ensure a detour, or at least a delay, in carrying out that primary mission. That appears in a number of passages that show Jesus talking about the necessity to first

suffer and die and be raised on the third day. Again, we are faced
with the fact that some passages in the Bible don't always fit together
very well. Did Jesus view his crucifixion as a step toward his mission
or see it as a tragic setback to what he originally intended to accom-
plish? A case can be made from the Bible for each of these positions,
and because it does involve the Bible we need to approach this matter with respectful consideration of both points of view.

The Gospels of Matthew, Mark, and Luke all show Jesus telling
his disciples three times about his death and resurrection. Here are
the three occasions as related in the Gospel of Matthew:

> From that time on Jesus began to show his disciples that he
> must go to Jerusalem and undergo great suffering at the hands
> of the elders and chief priests and scribes, and on the third day
> be raised. (16:21)

> As they were gathering in Galilee, Jesus said to them, "The Son
> of Man is going to be betrayed into human hands, and they will
> kill him, and on the third day he will be raised." And they were
> greatly distressed. (17:22)

> While Jesus was going up to Jerusalem, he took the twelve
> disciples aside by themselves, and said to them on the way,
> "See, we are going up to Jerusalem, and the Son of Man will
> be handed over to the chief priests and scribes, and they will
> condemn him to death; then they will hand him over to the
> Gentiles to be mocked and flogged and crucified; and on the
> third day he will be raised." (20:17–20)

As for where the allusion to three days came from, it was from
the story of Jonah (Matt 12:40):

> "Just as Jonah was three days and three nights in the belly of
> the sea monster, so for three days and three nights the Son of
> Man will be in the heart of the earth."

How could Jesus' death and resurrection fit in with a mission of
bringing in the kingdom? As we have seen, Matthew 13 says that he
was going to send his angels. But later, in a seeming adjustment for
the fact that Jesus did not bring in the kingdom during his lifetime,

that same gospel says instead that he would be coming with them (Matt 16:27):

> "For the Son of Man is to come with his angels in the glory of his Father and then he will repay everyone for what has been done."

The above is just one example of this theme that can be given from the gospels. Here is another (Matt 25:31):

> "When the Son of Man comes in his glory, and all the angels with him, then he will sit on the throne of his glory."

To examine this matter we need to ask what the purpose of the crucifixion was and who benefited from it. Let's first look at this from the viewpoint of the enemies of Jesus—proponents of the Temple system and officials of the Roman Empire. Some of them certainly saw a benefit in having out of the picture a person who sought to destroy the Temple system of sacrifice that they believed God required and which was also essential to their authority and livelihood. Even for some who were not leaders at the Temple, there would be a benefit in removing this harsh critic of some of their teachings and competitor for their own followers. And the Romans would have seen a benefit in eliminating a charismatic figure who posed a political threat by offering the hope of restoring the Davidic kingship.

The enemies of Jesus clearly benefited from his execution, but did anyone else? From the standpoint of Jesus, was there a purpose for the crucifixion? A reason is given in Mark 10:45:

> "For the Son of Man came not to be served but to serve, and to give his life a ransom for many."

Related to this, Luke 24:26 reconciles the death of Jesus with a conviction that it was necessary for the messiah to suffer. As part of an episode that we will look at in further detail in the next chapter, Luke 24:26 has the risen Jesus saying this to two disciples on the road to Emmaus:

> "Was it not necessary that the Messiah should suffer these things and then enter into his glory?"

But again, as we have seen, Jewish expectation was that the messiah would be a triumphal earthly king rather than a person put to death. Jesus confirmed that intention by seeking to fulfill Zech 9:9 with his entrance into Jerusalem. As for suffering and giving his life, Jesus had made clear that God is much too merciful to demand as an offering the suffering and death even of an animal, let alone a person.

From the standpoint of Jesus the crucifixion posed serious disadvantages, even apart from the agony of dying in that way. It delayed the fruition of what all the urgency was about—bringing in the kingdom; at the earliest, it couldn't happen until after the resurrection in three days' time.

A widely witnessed resurrection followed by God's cooperation in at last bringing in the new age would have been stunningly impressive. We will look more closely at the resurrection in the next chapter. However, it was not widely witnessed and was not followed by any dawn of a new age on earth. Although Jesus had absolutely promised that the kingdom would arrive within the lifetime of some persons who were then alive, they all died without seeing it happen. Within a few decades after Jesus' death not only were the Romans still in power and the kingdom of David still waiting to be restored, but Jerusalem had been devastated and the Temple destroyed.

If the crucifixion benefited no one except the enemies of Jesus, why say Jesus declared it as necessary? As we saw in Chapter 2, gospel writers sometimes showed more interest in telling a message favorable to Jesus than stating historical fact. This means that we need to consider the possibility that the passages that depict Jesus discussing the crucifixion and the kingdom afterward are a tradition that developed to explain why he died and why he failed to bring in the new age during his lifetime. Under this view, he died as atonement for the sins of the world. Although Jesus himself saw no need for blood sacrifice, there were still those who did, as we will see in the next chapter.

Not just the first three gospels but also the book of Acts explains that Jesus had not carried out his stated mission with the belief that he was going to come again. In fact, the book of Acts directly acknowledges the immediate earthly messianic hope by saying that the apostles asked the risen Jesus, "Lord, is this the time when you will restore the kingdom to Israel?" Then it justifies the nonarrival of the kingdom by saying Jesus told them the time wasn't theirs to know (Acts 1:6–7). In so doing, Acts turns a Jesus who had once been specific enough to promise people that they would see the kingdom in their lifetime into a Jesus who offers no specifics at all.

What the gospels say about the death of Jesus as atonement for sin and his return are both likely influenced by what Paul had written years before on those subjects. As we will see in the next chapter, Paul firmly believed in the necessity of blood sacrifice. Also, he had been teaching that the return of Jesus was imminent. As an example of that, in 1 Cor 10:11 Paul refers to "us, on whom the ends of the ages have come." And in Rom 13:11–12 he writes that "salvation is nearer to us now than when we became believers; the night is far gone, the day is near." However, the fact that Jesus had not returned posed a problem that required encouragement. In 1 Thess 4:13–18 Paul addresses this with a promise concerning believers who had already died without seeing the coming of the new age:

> But we do not want you to be uninformed, brothers and sisters, about those who have died, so that you may not grieve as others do who have no hope. For since we believe that Jesus died and rose again, even so, through Jesus, God will bring with him those who have died. For this we declare to you by the word of the Lord, that we who are alive, who are left until the coming of the Lord, will by no means precede those who have died. For the Lord himself, with a cry of command, with the archangel's call and with the sound of God's trumpet, will descend from heaven, and the dead in Christ will rise first. Then we who are alive, who are left, will be caught up in the clouds together with them to meet the Lord in the air; and so we will be with the Lord forever. Therefore encourage one another with these words.

Here Paul breaks with the Jewish tradition of his time that the restoration of life after death will be in a physical body on this earth. He foresees instead a transition to heaven "to be with the Lord forever." Some Bible scholars have expressed doubt that in this passage Paul actually meant to depict a U-turn of Christ in which he would return to gather believers and then turn around and lead them to heaven. However, taking the 1 Thessalonians passage literally is in keeping with Paul's understanding of what the new body of each believer will be like (1 Cor 15:48–49):

> As was the man of dust, so are those who are of the dust; and as is the man of heaven, so are those who are of heaven. Just as we have borne the image of the man of dust, we will also bear the image of the man of heaven.

Regardless, any interpretation of the 1 Thessalonians passage faces the broader problem of challenging credulity. In addressing this to "we who are alive" and his admonition to encourage one another with those words, Paul repeats the promise of Jesus that the new kingdom was to happen within the lifetime of some people who were then living. As we saw earlier in this chapter, the first three gospels show Jesus absolutely promising that his own generation would not pass away until that was fulfilled. However, if we think of people typically having children by the age of thirty, we now live in a time when more than sixty generations have since come and passed away. Perhaps even Paul had second thoughts, for that scenario in 1 Thessalonians appears only there, the earliest letter we have from him. He never mentions it again.

The discrepancies about the crucifixion and mission of Jesus leave us with needing to seriously consider a range of possibilities. As we examine for ourselves what meaning there might be to the crucifixion, it might be wise to look at something else the gospels relate Jesus as saying about it: that it was a disaster. In Matt 27:46 and Mark 15:34, the words *My God, my God, why have you forsaken me?* are not the words of someone willingly dying according to plan. If Jesus had not actually said this, drawn from Ps 22:1, there would have been no reason for gospel writers who were trying to find a noble meaning in his death to have made up those words of despair. Thus we have in Jesus' own words that the crucifixion was a tragic setback that served no purpose for him.

So how did the death of Jesus initially come to be seen as an act of intentional self-sacrifice, in clear contradiction of his own goals and teachings? For the details on that we need to go back to a time before any of the gospels were written and take a closer look at Paul.

Paul

Although Jesus was among the many Jews of his time who believed salvation comes through repentance alone, there were still Jews who believed that blood sacrifice was necessary. One of those was Paul, whose letters, or epistles, are the earliest portions of the New Testament to be written.

When discussing Paul, it is important to make clear which letters we are actually considering. Thirteen letters in the New Testament claim to be written by Paul. Of those, only seven are indisputably by him—Romans, 1 Corinthians, 2 Corinthians, Galatians, Philippians, 1 Thessalonians, and Philemon. Those that many New Testament scholars doubt were actually written by Paul and that are under varying levels of dispute are Ephesians, Colossians, 2 Thessalonians, 1 Timothy, 2 Timothy, and Titus. It is not within the scope of this book to give detailed reasons for believing that the authors of these works falsely claimed to be Paul to try to gain his authority for their own thoughts. However, some of the reasons these letters are considered inauthentic include differences of style and vocabulary from Paul's undisputed letters, an apparent historical setting that is later than Paul's time, and positions that contradict some of what Paul himself actually wrote. For purposes of this book we will consider only the seven undisputed letters.

No New Testament author writes about God's love with more eloquence than Paul. An example is Rom 8:38–39:

> For I am convinced that neither death, nor life, nor angels, nor rulers, nor things present, nor things to come, nor powers, nor height, nor depth, nor anything else in all creation, will be able to separate us from the love of God in Christ Jesus our Lord.

For Paul, that love is inseparably tied to his belief that salvation is made possible only through the death of Jesus. For a summary of Paul's message about Jesus' death, its meaning, and the events that followed it, we can look at 1 Cor 15:3–8:

For I handed on to you as of first importance what I had in turn received: that Christ died for our sins in accordance with the scriptures, and that he was buried, and that he was raised on the third day in accordance with the scriptures, and that he appeared to Cephas [Peter], then to the twelve. Then he appeared to more than five hundred brothers and sisters at one time, most of whom are still alive, though some have died. Then he appeared to James, then to all the apostles. Last of all, as to one untimely born, he appeared also to me.

Let's look at the points in the above passage one at a time. We'll begin with what it says about the resurrection, because that leads us to the call of Paul as an apostle.

Significantly, nowhere in the Bible is the resurrection itself actually described. We have only accounts of what happened later. Furthermore, the gospel records of the post-resurrection appearances of Jesus conflict in important ways.

Matthew and Mark place the post-resurrection appearances of Jesus to his apostles solely in Galilee. In Mark's gospel, Mary Magdalene, Mary the mother of James, and Salome encounter at the empty tomb a young man dressed in white. In Mark 16:7 he instructs them to tell Peter and the others that Jesus is going ahead of them to Galilee and that they will see him there. The Gospel of Matthew tells the same story with only minor differences, such as saying that the person in white was an angel. He gives the same instructions about Galilee as in Mark (Matt 28:6–7):

> "He is not here; for he has been raised, as he said. Come, see the place where he lay. Then go quickly and tell his disciples, 'He has been raised from the dead, and indeed he is going ahead of you to Galilee; there you will see him.' This is my message for you."

Matthew adds that after the women left the tomb Jesus appeared to them and asked them to tell the others to go on to Galilee where they would see him (Matt 28:8–10).

Mark 16:9 says that Jesus first appeared solely to Mary Magdalene. However, that is part of one of the additional endings to Mark that were possibly added because the earliest manuscripts do not end in a very satisfying way. They say that Jesus would be seen in Galilee but do not mention him actually being seen by anyone. Instead, they end abruptly, with fear and silence on the part of the women who saw the young man dressed in white at the tomb (Mark 16:8):

> So they went out and fled from the tomb, for terror and amaze-
> ment had seized them; and they said nothing to anyone, for
> they were afraid.

A complication with the resurrection stories in Matthew and Mark is that in the Gospel of Luke and the book of Acts Jesus appears not in Galilee but only in and near Jerusalem. In fact, in flat contradiction to the Galilee version, the book of Acts has the risen Jesus ordering his disciples not to leave Jerusalem (see Acts 1:4).

Luke says that on the same day that the tomb was found to be empty, two disciples were walking to the village of Emmaus about seven miles from Jerusalem when they were joined by Jesus. They did not immediately recognize him, and when they did he promptly disappeared before their eyes (Luke 24:28–31):

> As they came near the village to which they were going, he
> walked ahead as if he were going on. But they urged him
> strongly, saying, "Stay with us because it is almost evening and
> the day is now nearly over." So he went in to stay with them.
> When he was at the table with them, he took bread, blessed
> and broke it, and gave it to them. Then their eyes were opened,
> and they recognized him; and he vanished from their sight.

Luke then says that the pair returned to Jerusalem, found the eleven remaining apostles, told them what had happened, and learned that Jesus had also appeared to Simon Peter (Luke 24:33–34). In spite of the fact that Luke says Jesus was capable of simply vanishing, we have that report that he was material enough to break bread, and Luke later says that his disciples were able to touch him (Luke 24:38–39). Likewise, the Gospel of John says that the risen Jesus could pass through the walls of a locked room (John 20:19), but was also able to be touched, and that it was in touching Jesus that Thomas set aside his doubts (John 20:24–28).

That still leaves us with the Galilee-versus-Jerusalem discrepancy. John only complicates it further. As we have seen, in Matthew and Mark an angel tells Mary Magdalene that Jesus was not at the tomb but was going ahead to Galilee. However, John 20 says instead that the risen Jesus was at the tomb and appeared to Mary Magdalene there. The same chapter also says Jesus appeared twice to his disciples in a room that was presumably in Jerusalem, since the first visit was on the same day Mary Magdalene spoke with the disciples. Then John 21 tells us that Jesus appeared later to his disciples in Galilee along the shore of Lake Tiberias, also known as the Sea of Galilee.

It is understandable if you are feeling a bit bewildered at this point since, depending on the gospel, we have reports of the resurrected Jesus seen only in and near Jerusalem, or only in Galilee, or in both Jerusalem and Galilee. Also, the book of Acts says that the risen Jesus spent forty days with his apostles in Jerusalem, during which he spoke about the kingdom of God (Acts 1:3). If so, it is inexplicable why his post-resurrection teachings would not be important enough to warrant an extensive narrative such as that of his teachings before his death. Surely his apostles would have done their best to record, cherish, and pass down every word. Instead, those forty days are all dismissed in just a few verses at the beginning of Acts. That and the differences among the gospels raise the question of why no resurrection appearance at all was so memorable that the details were recorded and passed down consistently. Instead, what we have suggests a determination to have people believe Jesus rose from the dead but considerable differences of opinion about what to say about it. The situation is similar to the authors of the Gospels of Matthew and Luke both writing that Jesus had a virgin birth in Bethlehem, but saying it only in highly contradictory stories.

Another significant issue with the resurrection is the matter of how many people are said to have seen the risen Jesus. As we saw in 1 Corinthians, Paul said the resurrected Jesus had been seen by more than five hundred people at a time. However, none of the gospels mention that. Since that would have been too spectacular an event to be omitted, it appears likely that by the time the gospels were written such an account was not taken seriously. And that calls into question why the risen Jesus was not more widely seen. It seems reasonable that if God were to actually do something as impressive as raise Jesus from the dead, he would have wanted him seen by as many people as possible. For instance, an appearance witnessed by everyone at the Temple of a physically resurrected Jesus would have provided startling evidence that he had a unique nature and authority. The best explanation for the fact that nothing like that happened seems to be that any sightings of a risen Jesus were actually visionary experiences reported by only a very few.

That brings us to the call of Paul to apostleship. I use the word "call" instead of "conversion" because conversion implies a move to another religion. In the time of Paul, there was no separate religion called Christianity. Just as Judaism already had a variety of sects within it, there was now a new one—the Jesus movement.

The two best-known and most dramatic descriptions of Paul's call are found not in his writings but in Acts. They say Paul, known then as Saul, was doing all he could to persecute the followers of Jesus when he had an encounter with the risen Jesus. Here is the version from Acts 9:3–8:

> Now as he was going along and approaching Damascus, suddenly a light from heaven flashed around him, He fell to the ground and heard a voice saying to him, "Saul, Saul, why do you persecute me?" He asked, "Who are you, Lord?" The reply came, "I am Jesus, whom you are persecuting. But get up and enter the city, and you will be told what to do." The men who were traveling with him stood speechless because they heard the voice but saw no one. Saul got up from the ground, and though his eyes were open, he could see nothing; so they led him by the hand and brought him into Damascus.

Later in Acts we have the same story, presented as if in words told by Paul himself, but with his companions seeing a light but hearing nothing (Acts 22:6–11). Both versions say that Paul's sight was restored after an encounter with a man in Damascus named Ananias. Acts 9 says that Jesus appeared to Ananias in a vision and told him how to find Paul. Ananias protests, saying that he has heard that Paul has done much evil against the followers of Jesus in Jerusalem. Then the episode concludes (Acts 9:15–19):

> But the Lord said to him, "Go, for he is an instrument whom I have chosen to bring my name before Gentiles and kings and

before the people of Israel; I myself will show him how much he must suffer for the sake of my name." So Ananias went and entered the house. He laid his hands on Saul and said, "Brother Saul, the Lord Jesus, who appeared to you on your way here, has sent me so that you may regain your sight and be filled with the Holy Spirit." And immediately something like scales fell from his eyes, and his sight was restored. Then he got up and was baptized, and after taking some food, he regained his strength.

The experience on the road to Damascus is described only in Acts. Nowhere in his writings does Paul say anything so specific. Paul wrote of other major events in his life, and as we will see he angrily defended his validity as an apostle. But as for saying something occurred on the Damascus road, there is nothing. Since that would be the single most important event enhancing Paul's credibility as a representative of Jesus, it seems very strange that if such a thing happened he would not have specifically mentioned it in his letters. Instead, in 1 Cor 9:1 he says simply that he had seen Jesus. Beyond that, he makes only two brief mentions of his call. We have already looked at the first, in which Paul says that after appearing to others Jesus also appeared to him (1 Cor 15:8).

The 1 Corinthians 15 narrative about those to whom Jesus was said to have appeared poses some problems. For instance, Paul says that Jesus appeared not just to the apostles but also to Jesus' brother James (1 Cor 15:5–7). Neither Acts nor the gospels have a record of Jesus appearing to that James, although that does not necessarily mean that he didn't. We have already observed that the gospel writers apparently found the reference to Jesus appearing to five hundred people at a time not credible enough to mention.

Paul's only remaining mention of his call is in Galatians and is even less specific than 1 Corinthians about the encounter. However, it is much more specific about what Paul understood it to mean about himself. In Galatians Paul does not even use the word "appeared" in reference to Jesus but just says that God chose "to reveal his Son to me, so that I might proclaim him among the Gentiles" (Gal 1:16). How that revelation took place is left unsaid. But, significantly, Paul expresses an understanding that God had set him apart for this even before he was born (see Gal 1:15).

The only other part of the 1 Corinthians 15 passage that we have yet to consider is what Paul says about Jesus dying as a remedy for sin in accordance with the scriptures. In 1 Cor 15.3 Paul makes clear that he was one of those who still believed blood sacrifice was necessary for the forgiveness of sin, and also that he believed Jesus died as such a sacrifice for the sins of others.

In the 1 Corinthians 15 passage Paul twice uses the phrase "in accordance with the scriptures." That would have meant the Hebrew Bible, since the New Testament did not yet exist.

One mention of "in accordance with the scriptures" refers to Jesus being raised on the third day. In this case, Paul may well have been referring to the story of Jonah being three days in the belly of the sea monster. However, another possibility is a verse from Hosea. Although it refers to "us" rather than "him," and is part of a passage that promises assistance from God that is likened to a spring shower, some came to see it as foretelling the resurrection (Hos 6:2):

> After two days he will revive us; on the third day he will raise us
> up, that we may live before him.

As for the other occurrence of "in accordance with the scriptures," regarding the crucifixion of Jesus, Paul may have been referring to Psalm 22. This verse mentions someone whose clothing was divided by casting lots (22:18), as all four gospels say happened to Jesus. Furthermore, in saying on the cross "My God, my God, why have you forsaken me?" Jesus was quoting the first verse of that psalm.

It seems likely that Paul also may especially have had in mind the suffering servant song in Isaiah. It is rather long—fifteen verses. But it is so important that, with some paragraph divisions for readability purposes, let us take a look at all of it (Isa 52:13–53:12):

> See, my servant shall prosper; he shall be exalted and lifted up,
> and shall be very high. Just as there were many who were aston-
> ished at him—so marred was his appearance, beyond human
> semblance, and his form beyond that of mortals—so he shall

startle many nations; kings shall shut their mouths because of him; for that which had not been told them they shall see, and that which they had not heard they shall contemplate.

Who has believed what we have heard? And to whom has the arm of the LORD been revealed? For he grew up before him like a young plant, and like a root out of dry ground; he had no form or majesty that we should look at him, nothing in his appearance that we should desire him. He was despised and rejected by others; a man of suffering and acquainted with infirmity; and as one from whom others hide their faces he was despised, and we held him of no account.

Surely he has borne our infirmities and carried our diseases; yet we accounted him stricken, struck down by God, and afflicted. But he was wounded for our transgressions, crushed for our iniquities; upon him was the punishment that made us whole, and by his bruises we are healed. All we like sheep have gone astray; we have all turned to our own way, and the LORD has laid on him the iniquity of us all. He was oppressed, and he was afflicted, yet he did not open his mouth; like a lamb that is led to the slaughter, and like a sheep that before its shearers is silent, so he did not open his mouth. By a perversion of justice he was taken away. Who could have imagined his future? For he was cut off from the land of the living, stricken for the transgression of my people. They made his grave with the wicked and his tomb with the rich, although he had done no violence, and there was no deceit in his mouth.

Yet it was the will of the LORD to crush him with pain. When you make his life an offering for sin, he shall see his offspring, and shall prolong his days; through him the will of the LORD shall prosper. Out of his anguish he shall see light; he shall find satisfaction through his knowledge. The righteous one, my servant, shall make many righteous, and he shall bear their iniquities. Therefore I will allot him a portion with the great, and he shall divide the spoil with the strong; because he poured out himself to death, and was numbered with the transgressors; yet he bore the sin of many, and made intercession for the transgressors.

It is easy to understand how someone who thought of Jesus as a blood sacrifice for sin could see this portion of Isaiah as a prophecy of it. However, there are several problems with this view. First, the suffering servant was not executed; he was diseased, with an appearance that caused others to hide their faces from him. Also, he would live to see his offspring. And, significantly, this passage never says that the suffering servant was the messiah. It is hard to reconcile all these things to a prophecy of the death of Jesus.

In looking at Isaiah's song of the suffering servant, we also need to look at the time and context in which it was written. It was written hundreds of years before the birth of Jesus to offer encouragement to Jews who were in exile in Babylonia. As such, it seems that the suffering servant may be a poetic personification of Israel as a whole, which had suffered enough through conquest and then captivity to atone for whatever sins of its individual people had led to that situation. And in fact the book of Isaiah itself indicates that the servant is indeed Israel. The song of the suffering servant is one of four servant songs in Isaiah. For the others, see Isa 42:1–4; 49:1–6; and 50:4–11. In the second song we see who the servant is (Isa 49:3):

And he [the LORD] said to me, "You are my servant, Israel, in whom I will be glorified."

The Gospel of Matthew also sees Jesus as a fulfillment of the Isaiah passage that Paul may have had in mind. But Matthew views the Isaiah passage simply in terms of Jesus' role as a healer with no reference to his death (Matt 8:14–17):

When Jesus entered Peter's house, he saw his mother-in-law lying in bed with a fever; he touched her hand, and the fever left her, and she got up and began to serve him. That evening they brought to him many who were possessed with demons; and he cast out the spirits with a word, and cured all who were sick. This was to fulfill what had been spoken through the prophet Isaiah, "He took our infirmities and bore our diseases"

Strongly related to Paul's understanding of the death of Jesus as a blood sacrifice is the description of the Last Supper, the observance of which is now commonly called by various names such as the

Sacrament of the Lord's Supper, Eucharist, and Holy Communion. The narrative of the Last Supper did not come from anyone who was with Jesus at the last meal that he shared with his apostles, all of whom—*as his disciples*—probably agreed with him that blood sacrifice is unnecessary. Instead, the Last Supper narrative came later—from Paul, someone who had never met Jesus during his lifetime. Paul says it himself (1 Cor 11:23–26):

> For I received from the Lord what I also handed on to you, that the Lord Jesus on the night when he was betrayed took a loaf of bread, and when he had given thanks, he broke it and said, "This is my body that is for you. Do this in remembrance of me."
>
> In the same way he took the cup also, after supper, saying, "This cup is the new covenant in my blood. Do this as often as you drink it in remembrance of me."

In addition to supporting the view of salvation through blood sacrifice that Jesus rejected, something else seems very out of place about Paul's presentation of the Last Supper. The thought that Jesus would have asked his followers to even symbolically drink his blood is startling in light of the Jewish dietary prohibition against consuming blood, a requirement that applies even today in the proper kosher preparation of food. In Gen 9:4, God tells Noah that no meat is to be eaten that still has blood in it. That is the basis of one of the so-called Noahide laws, which applied to everyone, Jew and Gentile alike. In fact, Acts 15:20 shows James the brother of Jesus saying that one of the few restrictions placed on Gentile believers was that they abstain from blood.

For Jews, the rule about blood was emphasized as a dietary law, one expression of which is Lev 7:26–27:

> You must not eat any blood whatever, either of bird or animal, in any of your settlements. Any one of you who eats any blood shall be cut off from your kin.

Jesus and his apostles, as practicing Jews, would have been vividly aware at each meal of this necessity of avoiding the consumption of blood. Since consuming blood was a cause for revulsion, it is very difficult to imagine that Jesus would have used the occasion of a meal to say anything even figuratively about drinking his.

Some commentaries on the Bible assume that the description of the Last Supper began with an oral tradition from Jesus' disciples. However, as we have seen, Paul said he got it in a revelation from Jesus and implies that no one else had heard about it until it was "handed on" by him. This is in keeping with his insistence that what he taught came from no human being (Gal 1:11–12):

> For I want you to know, brothers and sisters, that the gospel
> that was proclaimed by me is not of human origin; for I did
> not receive it from a human source, nor was I taught it, but I
> received it through a revelation of Jesus Christ.

We know from Paul that by the time he wrote 1 Corinthians the Jesus fellowship in Corinth was already engaging in an observance of the Lord's Supper according to Paul's teachings. Paul just didn't believe that they were doing it with the proper dedication (see 1 Cor 11:20–22). The fact that the first three gospels reflect Paul's depiction of the Last Supper suggests that when those gospels were later written the practice was already widespread.

For reasons not entirely clear, the Gospel of John, considered by many scholars to be the last of the canonical gospels to be written, says that Jesus had a final meal with his disciples but says nothing about it as an institution to be continued in his memory. Since the author of the Gospel of John seems aware of earlier gospels, that absence remains a mystery. Including the Last Supper as an institution by Jesus would have reinforced that gospel's understanding of the mission of Jesus. One reason for the omission may be that since the details of the Last Supper apparently came from Paul, the author of the fourth gospel may not have found them credible. Instead, he presents the same concepts of consuming the body and blood of Jesus as part of a lesson that he says Jesus taught at Capernaum, and which his disciples found hard to accept (see John 6:48–60).

Ultimately, the revelation that Paul says he received from Jesus about the Last Supper seems to be more a reflection of Paul than Jesus. It dramatically contradicts what Jesus taught about forgiveness through repentance alone but agrees with Paul's belief that blood sacrifice was still required.

According to Paul, how does one obtain the benefits of the death of Jesus? Unlike John the Baptist and Jesus, nowhere does Paul say to repent. In fact, the word "repent" does not appear even once in any of his letters. The word "repentance" does appear, three times, and all as a consequence of something rather than in reference to an intentional decision. In Rom 2:4 repentance comes as a consequence of God's kindness. The other two references to repentance are in 2 Cor 7:9–10, where repentance is a consequence of "godly grief" that points toward the path to salvation. For Paul that path is simply to have faith and believe. He sums up his position in Rom 3:21–25a:

> But now, apart from the law, the righteousness of God has
> been disclosed, and is attested by the law and the prophets, the
> righteousness of God through faith in Jesus Christ for all who
> believe. For there is no distinction, since all have sinned and
> fallen short of the glory of God; they are now justified by his
> grace, as a gift, through the redemption that is in Christ Jesus,
> whom God put forward as a sacrifice of atonement, by his
> blood, effective through faith.

Here we see all the key elements of Paul's message concerning salvation. He says Jesus was a blood sacrifice of atonement, and to obtain the benefits of this sacrifice one must have faith in Jesus Christ. Simply believe, and then salvation comes by grace. Here is another example from Romans, this time 10:9–10:

> Because if you confess with your lips that Jesus is Lord and
> believe in your heart that God raised him from the dead, you
> will be saved. For one believes with the heart and is so justified,
> and one confesses with the mouth and is so saved.

Part of Paul's understanding of salvation seems to come from being locked into a rigid view concerning keeping the Jewish law, the Torah. For him Jesus provides a necessary means of grace, since otherwise Paul sees any shortcoming at all in complying with the Torah as fatal (Gal 3:10):

> For all who rely on the works of the law are under a curse, for it
> is written, "Cursed is everyone who does not observe and obey
> all the things written in the book of the law."

The curse that Paul mentions is a reference to Deut 27:26, and for him the remedy for it goes back to the old Aaronite priesthood's insistence that blood sacrifice is the only solution.

As we saw in Chapter 6, those who believed in the necessity of Temple sacrifice saw the death of the animal as a substitutionary atonement for the sinner making the offering. Thus, it is easy to understand how Paul made a transition from that to seeing Jesus as a substitutionary atonement for all believers. For him, the death of Jesus on the cross was the ultimate and sufficient blood sacrifice that removes the sting of falling short of the demands of the Torah, but only for those who believe.

Of course, the problem here is that Jesus proclaimed something else—a God of such great love and mercy that he requires not the shedding of blood but only repentance. In fact, even after including Paul's version of the Last Supper, the author of the Gospel of Luke ultimately could not accept Paul's view of the crucifixion. With no suggestion of substitutionary blood sacrifice, Luke says that the risen Jesus told his disciples to proclaim to all nations in his name that forgiveness of sins comes through repentance (Luke 24:47).

Jesus taught that, as important as reaching out to God in repentance is, that alone is not sufficient—and it is certainly not sufficient just to believe something. We must also express love and mercy to others in offering repentance, forgiveness, and reconciliation to one another. Although Paul wrote eloquently about God's love, Jesus took the understanding of that love to a much higher and more profound level than even Paul, with his thinking locked in blood sacrifice, could comprehend. Jesus said his followers need to look to God for grace, but not God alone; they also need to offer grace to one another.

How did Paul move so far from what Jesus had taught? As we saw earlier in a passage from Galatians, he said his message about the significance of Jesus was "not of human origin" (Gal 1:11). But if it really was from the risen Jesus, Paul's view of salvation should not have been so different from Jesus' message of repentance in the first three gospels, which presumably derive from oral accounts by those who had known Jesus.

This brings us to the matter of the opposition that Paul encountered. We see from Paul's letters that his teachings about

Jesus were far from free of controversy. Significantly, Paul complains about people who were causing some of his converts to turn away from what he taught (Gal 1:6–9). What they were saying that offended him seemed to go well beyond any issue over outreach to Gentiles. His outrage, defensiveness, and scathing mention of "a different gospel" (Gal 1:6) indicate that he was under serious theological attack. Obviously, this was from teachers with an authority recognized by those they met. At that very early time in the Jesus movement, that level of respect would most likely have been granted to visitors from the Jerusalem church, bearing teachings handed down through those who had actually known Jesus. In fact, Paul says with disgust that there had been people who came "from those who were supposed to be acknowledged leaders," but then adds that "those leaders contributed nothing to me" (Gal 2:6). And in 2 Corinthians he chastises his readers for submitting to the views of "false apostles, deceitful workers, disguising themselves as apostles of Christ" (2 Cor 11:13). Who were they? He sarcastically refers to them as "super-apostles" (2 Cor 11:5), a term which in that time could only have referred to those from the Jerusalem church.

As we have seen, Paul takes great pride in not accepting any human authority, even if they were people who had been taught firsthand by Jesus himself. Paul is so closed to any views but his own that he writes that even any angel from heaven who dares to disagree with him should be damned (see Gal 1:8). For Paul this came with a price—the frustration of dealing with those who insisted that Paul needed to be corrected because they found some of his positions impossible to reconcile with their understanding of the Jesus they had personally known.

The ongoing observance of the Lord's Supper up to our own day, depicting Jesus as a sacrifice for sin and based on a unique teaching of Paul, may help explain why Christians have typically been distracted from what Jesus taught about forgiveness through repentance. But that does not explain how Jesus came to be seen as a deity.

The gospels and Paul all refer to Jesus as the son of God, but that was a term that traditionally had nothing to do with actually being God. The Davidic king was considered to be God's son, as someone presumably guided by God, but no one thought he was divine. We can see this symbolic relationship in 2 Samuel, where God promises that there will always be a king from David's line (2 Sam 7:14):

> I will be a father to him and he shall be a son to me.

Nowhere in the first three gospels does Jesus claim to be God. Also, Paul consistently makes a distinction between Jesus and God. For instance, Paul never says that Jesus rose from the dead by some divine power of his own. Instead, he says he was raised by God. A typical example showing his distinction between God and Jesus is 1 Cor 6:14:

> And God raised the Lord and will also raise us by his power.

Paul comes closest to saying that Jesus is divine in Phil 2:5–7:

> Let the same mind be in you that was in Christ Jesus, who,
> though he was in the form of God, did not regard equality with
> God as something to be exploited, but emptied himself, taking
> the form of a slave, being born in human likeness.

But then Paul immediately steps back to draw a distinction between Jesus and God by saying "God also highly exalted him" (Phil 2:9) so that "every tongue should confess that Jesus Christ is Lord to the glory of God the Father" (Phil 2:11).

Paul also makes the distinction between God the Father and Jesus as Lord in 1 Cor 8:6:

> Yet for us there is one God, the Father, from whom are all
> things and for whom we exist, and one Lord, Jesus Christ,
> through whom are all things and through whom we exist.

Clearly, even in seeing Jesus as a fundamental force in the world, Paul views Jesus Christ as Lord and God the Father as separate. Other instances can be given, but we will end our examples with 1 Cor 11:3:

> But I want you to understand that Christ is the head of every
> man, and the husband is the head of his wife, and God is the
> head of Christ.

Here Paul expresses his view that Christ ranks above every man, that a man ranks above his wife, and that God ranks above Christ and is thus superior to him. Although for Paul Jesus was "highly exalted," he clearly draws a distinction between Jesus and God. As for the concept of Jesus as part of a divine Trinity, we will look at that in the next two chapters.

In Paul we see the foundations of Christianity as primarily a Gentile religion, and also as a religion that largely ignores what Jesus taught about repentance—a religion that instead sees his death as sacrificial atonement for sin. The outreach to the Gentiles was to prove essential to the future of the Jesus movement, because it was already becoming clear that most Jews rejected it. The need to enlist Gentiles to help the movement grow led to a major change of emphasis in the Gospel of Matthew. As we saw in Chapter 1, Matthew's Jesus made clear that what he was offering was only for Jews. But in the next-to-last verse of that gospel the author depicts the risen Jesus as commanding his followers to "make disciples of all nations" (Matt 28:19). Thus, writing after Paul opened the Jesus movement to Gentiles, and decades after the death of Jesus, Matthew too says Gentiles were encouraged into the fold.

We have seen how the Jesus movement was opened to the Gentiles even before there was a separate religion called Christianity. To see how Jesus came to be viewed as divine, we need to look in detail at the fourth gospel and another writer who believed in blood sacrifice.

 **John**

The Gospel of John completes the New Testament's transition to seeing Jesus as a Christ deity fully in command of his destiny.

The fourth gospel differs so fundamentally from the first three gospels that we are left with the question of which approach more correctly presents the historical Jesus of Nazareth. What the first three gospels say Jesus taught about salvation through repentance and his mission to bring in an imminent new age on earth is totally missing from John. The omission is so systematic and complete that someone unfamiliar with the Gospels of Matthew, Mark, and Luke would be unlikely to sense anything is missing, except for John's presentation of John the Baptist. As we shall later see, on that point even someone unfamiliar with the first three gospels could well sense that the story may not be quite as it appears.

With so much of importance resting on whether the first three gospels or the Gospel of John most correctly presents the Jesus of history, let's look at the evidence.

First, many biblical scholars agree that the Gospels of Matthew, Mark, and Luke were written before John. And there is general agreement that they drew on sources that were even earlier. Thus, they are closer to the events they describe. In fact, there was a tradition in the early church that the Gospel of Mark is based on information gathered as a traveling companion of Peter, perhaps as a person who translated Peter's sermons from Aramaic into the Greek of his listeners.

The author of the Gospel of John was likely aware that other gospels had been written before his. If so he would have known that they show Jesus proclaiming forgiveness of sins through repentance alone. Even though it led to some awkwardness in their presentation of Jesus' mission, all the other gospel writers mentioned it. However, if the author of John was aware of it, he was determined to erase, without a trace, the Jesus who proclaimed forgiveness through repentance and replace him with a Christ without whose sacrifice on the cross no forgiveness was possible. Unlike the other gospels, the words "repent" and "repentance" never appear in the Gospel of John.

The question is, was the author of the Gospel of John just not aware of Jesus proclaiming forgiveness through repentance, or was he aware of it and deleted it intentionally? There is evidence that it was intentional.

John the Baptist was such a significant figure that John the gospel writer could not leave him out of the story, but this created an awkward situation. As we have already seen, according to the earlier gospels, in keeping with the mikveh practices of his day John the Baptist was offering a baptism of repentance for the forgiveness of sins. Furthermore, he was doing this even before Jesus appeared on the scene to begin his ministry, and Jesus clearly approved of what the Baptist was doing. This seemed to have caused a serious problem for John the gospel writer. To admit that forgiveness by repentance alone was possible would destroy his premise that forgiveness was possible only through the blood sacrifice of Jesus himself.

To deal with the problem, John the gospel writer turned the message of John the Baptist upside down. Instead of urging repentance and proclaiming Jesus the harbinger of God's kingdom on earth, this gospel's John the Baptist proclaims Jesus a pending blood sacrifice (John 1:29):

> The next day he saw Jesus coming toward him and declared,
> "Here is the Lamb of God who takes away the sin of the world!"

Only the Gospel of John calls Jesus the Lamb of God. And, compared to the other gospels, it also moves the crucifixion of Jesus up a day to place it on the day of preparation for Passover. The symbolism is obvious, since that was the day when Jews would bring their Passover lambs to the Temple for slaughter.

This left the author of the Gospel of John with the problem of explaining why John the Baptist was baptizing in the Jordan. Saying, as do all the other gospels, that he was offering a baptism of repentance for the forgiveness of sins would have made a Lamb of God unnecessary. Instead, he says that John the Baptist came baptizing with water so that Jesus "might be revealed to Israel" (John 1:31). That's very strange. If the Baptist simply wanted people to see Jesus or learn about Jesus he could point out Jesus or preach about Jesus. But baptism makes sense only in the purposeful and historical context in which it is mentioned in the other gospels. There are specific reasons for a mikveh immersion, but to have someone revealed to you was not and never has been one of them. Mikveh practices would never have required anyone to go totally under water to learn about Jesus. In harsh contrast to the other gospels, the author of the Gospel of John erases the message by John the Baptist and Jesus of forgiveness through repentance in a way that is very hard to explain if it was not his intent.

As might be expected, John also deletes the Lord's Prayer from the gospel traditions. In saying that people should ask God to forgive them as they forgive others, Jesus again bypassed any need for blood sacrifice. That was something that the author of the Gospel of John apparently could not tolerate.

By not saying that John the Baptist and Jesus urged repentance to prepare for an imminent new age on earth, John the gospel writer opened the way to explain why the messianic age never arrived. Only in John's gospel does Jesus tell Pilate that his kingdom is not of this world (John 18:36). However, as we have seen, the Jewish hope for a messiah was for a new Davidic reign on earth, and Jesus told people they would see the new age on earth in their lifetime.

In presenting Jesus as a blood sacrifice, the author of the Gospel of John is in agreement with Paul. However, Paul wrote years before any of the gospels and was echoing a belief about the importance of sacrifice still held by many Jews of his time. It is much harder to understand the motivation of the author of the Gospel of John, who wrote after the other gospels had put the position of Jesus on forgiveness and a merciful God firmly on the record.

But this gospel's most radical break with the writers of the other three gospels, and with Paul, is to say that Jesus is God. John has no nativity story because the human form of the Jesus he was proclaiming didn't concern him. Instead, he begins his gospel by saying Jesus is the divine preexistent Word through whom all things were made (John 1:1–3a, 14):

In the beginning was the Word, and the Word was with God
and the Word was God. He was in the beginning with God. All
things came into being through him, and without him not one
thing came into being. . . . And the Word became flesh and
lived among us, as we have seen his glory, the glory of a father's
only son, full of grace and truth.

Did Jesus see himself as God? Only in the Gospel of John is Jesus
represented as saying yes, and saying it again and again. In keeping
with the proclamation at the beginning of the gospel, John's Jesus
definitely sees himself as preexistent (John 17:5):

"So now, Father, glorify me with your own presence with the
glory that I had in your presence before the world existed."

John 10:30 has Jesus saying, "The Father and I are one." And later
in John he is shown as emphasizing to his disciples his unity with the
Father several times in only five verses (John 14:7–11):

"If you know me, you will know my Father also. From now on
you do know him and have seen him."
    Philip said to him, "Lord, show us the Father, and we will be
satisfied."
    Jesus said to him, "Have I been with you all this time, Philip,
and you still do not know me? Whoever has seen me has seen
the Father. How can you say, 'Show us the Father'? Do you
not believe that I am in the Father and the Father is in me?
The words that I say to you I do not speak on my own; but the
Father who dwells in me does his works. Believe me that I am
in the Father and the Father is in me; but if you do not, then
believe because of the works themselves."

Other examples can be given, but the point is made. In the
Gospel of John, and only in the Gospel of John, is Jesus presented
as seeing himself as God and wanting his disciples to have no
doubt about it. However, there is a problem with the view of Jesus,
a Jew, thinking of himself as divine. It can be summed up in one
word, Shema. For hundreds of years before the time of Jesus right
up until today, the Shema has been the primary faith statement

of the Jewish religion. Its first verse is Deut 6:4, commonly said in this way:

Hear, O Israel: the Lord is our God, the Lord is One!

Jews traditionally recite these words in Hebrew daily and again each night before sleep. They are repeated during prayers. They are an essential part of worship liturgies. They proclaim Judaism as a strictly monotheistic religion. And in affirming the uniqueness and singularity of God they are also an affirmation of the covenant establishing God's special relationship to Jews. They are the reason that Jews were willing to give up their lives rather than surrender to pagan cult worship of some Roman emperors as gods.

The Gospel of John itself confirms that Jews view claiming to be God as a dreadful heresy. John 10:33 says that Jesus was threatened with stoning as a blasphemer because some people believed he was making that claim for himself. But none of the gospel accounts of the trial of Jesus show his accusers condemning him for actually saying he was God, but instead the son of God. As we have already seen, that was a term for an earthly Davidic king. John 19:14 shows that even Pilate understood the distinction, for in a sarcastic reply to those who complained that Jesus claimed to be the son of God, Pilate said not "Here is your God!" but "Here is your King!"

It appears that the author of the Gospel of John was likely a Gentile. For if he was a Jew he would have realized that, as a Jew, Jesus could not have even conceived of violating the Shema by calling himself equal to God, let alone allowed himself to be addressed as God. And if his disciples, all of them Jews, thought that he actually made that claim, they would have seen him as a heretic and quickly abandoned him.

Some Christians of today may say there should be no problem here, since Christianity teaches a single God of which Jesus is one of three aspects. However, the doctrine of the Trinity did not exist in Jesus' time, even if Jesus as a Jew would have accepted it, and Jews have never accepted it. Thus, we are back where we started.

Most importantly, consider what Jesus himself said when asked what the greatest commandment is. Before quoting the commandment in Deut 6:5 to love God with our whole heart, Jesus prefaced it with Deut 6:4 in the following passage from Mark 12:28–29:

> One of the scribes came near and heard them disputing with one another, and seeing that he answered them well, he asked him, "Which commandment is the first of all?"
>
> Jesus answered, "The first is, 'Hear, O Israel, the Lord our God, the Lord is one.'"

Thus, Jesus saw an acknowledgement of God's unique singularity as an inseparable part of the greatest commandment.

Finally, not only do none of the first three gospels show Jesus saying he was God, but they all have him firmly saying he was not. For instance, Mark 10:18 quotes Jesus as saying, "Why do you call me good? No one is good but God alone." Obviously, he did not think of himself as a deity and took scolding offense at the thought that anyone might see him that way. He is shown as making the same point in Matt 19:17 and Luke 18:19. In doing so he is saying with humility that he, too, was a man of human imperfection.

As with his apparent replacement of the teachings of Jesus concerning repentance with his own ideas, here again the author of the Gospel of John seems to have placed his own views first. Seeing Jesus or any other human being as divine would be, for Jesus or any Jew of his time or ours, simply impossible. Asserting the divinity of Jesus by putting words in Jesus' mouth only adds to the questions about that gospel's historical credibility.

It is undeniable that the author of John wrote with great eloquence and passion. However, as we have seen, in doing so he creates a figure that Jesus of Nazareth would hardly have recognized as being based on him. Also, some of John's eloquence is really less useful and profound than it seems. For example, many people consider the most powerful verse in any of the gospels to be John 3:16:

> For God so loved the world that he gave his only Son, so that everyone who believes in him may not perish but may have eternal life.

The passage goes on to say that those who do not believe in him are condemned. John 3:16 and related verses have been among those used to claim that Christians alone have a monopoly on salvation and, by extension, that the church has a monopoly on the truth. Sadly, this has often led to supposed justification for great cruelty in demanding that people convert to Christianity or recant certain views. The author of the Gospel of John later reinforces his message that only Christians can obtain God's favor, especially with John 14:6, in which he relates Jesus as saying that no one comes to the Father except through him.

Similar wording that nonbelievers are condemned also found its way into one of the additional endings of the Gospel of Mark (16:16), perhaps written sometime in the late second or perhaps even early third century. However, the Gospels of Matthew and Luke, as well as the earliest manuscripts of Mark, do not have that passage.

As for its usefulness, John 3:16 says not a word about *what* must be believed about Jesus. Presumably, the author means that Jesus is God and died on the cross as a blood offering for the sins of the world. But as we have seen, the author of the Gospel of John totally ignores the fact that Jesus taught a far different and more merciful understanding of forgiveness and reconciliation, and he clearly wants everyone else to ignore Jesus on this as well. Some Bible commentators have said that the likelihood that the Gospel of John is the least historically accurate gospel is offset by its having great spiritual truth. In fact, it could hardly be more dismissive of values that Jesus of Nazareth held dear.

The author of the Gospel of John may have felt that his gospel would replace any others and would become the only one read. Instead, his was gathered into a collection with the first three, and its differences with them are obvious and substantial. So how did the position in the Gospel of John about salvation and the nature and mission of Jesus come to be accepted as Christian orthodoxy? For the answer to that we first need to look at the two most important creeds of the Christian faith.

10 Creeds

As we have seen, anyone setting out in the early years of Christianity to decide what the official doctrine should be could choose from several options. Which doctrines would emerge victorious—salvation by repentance to a God of mercy, or salvation by the blood sacrifice of Jesus to satisfy a stern God of justice? Jesus as God, or Jesus as a man who, in the sense of the kings of Israel, was considered a son of God? Jesus as a revolutionary seeking an immediate earthly kingship, or Jesus as a selfless offering to make eventual heavenly rewards available to others? And those were just some of the issues in debate.

To get an idea of the tension about beliefs and how early in the Jesus movement it started, one need only look at the letters of Paul. As we have already seen, he warns against false teachers. But, of course, those he complains about felt that the true false teacher was Paul.

Any thought that the differences in beliefs were simply those of Paul versus the leaders of the Jerusalem church would be a gross oversimplification. For as the years passed, the conflicts only worsened. There were the Ebionites, who denied the virgin birth, saw Paul as a heretic, and said that the Jesus movement should be open only to circumcised Jews. There were the Gnostics, who believed that the material world was created by someone less than God and that Jesus taught secret knowledge (*gnosis* in Greek) to be liberated from it. There was a man named Marcion who totally rejected the Jewish foundations of the Jesus movement and said that the creator God of the Hebrew Bible was a vengeful Being completely different from the God proclaimed by Jesus. There were other groups as well, having within them people who added their own variations to what they believed. And they all thought of themselves as having the one true faith. It was a time when what would eventually become the foundational beliefs of Christianity was far from obvious.

One might think that to sort this out, it was only necessary to check these beliefs against the New Testament. But as we have seen, the books of the New Testament are far from consistent on several key points. Also, although the books that are now in the New Testament were all written by the second century, they had a lot of company in the competition to be included. There were many other works claiming to be legitimate gospels, epistles, acts, and apocalypses. Early church leaders found that identifying and culling out forgeries as best as possible during those times, and also eliminating works considered heretical or unacceptable for other reasons, was such a long and disputed process that the final New Testament canon that we recognize today was not agreed upon until the Third Council of Carthage in 397 CE.

Standards had to be set. A major effort to reach a consensus came from the First Council of Nicaea in what is present-day Iznik, Turkey. It was called in 325 CE by Emperor Constantine. He is said to have become a Christian after believing that the Christian God had given him a vision in 312 CE offering to help him win the Battle of Milvian Bridge, a main route over the Tiber River. That victory made him the uncontested ruler of the Roman Empire.

The most significant controversy of the Council concerned a doctrinal conflict between the supporters of two men from Alexandria. One was a priest named Arius who had been teaching that God is ultimately unknowable and that since Christ was known, he had to have been created, although before the creation of the world. In that sense, Arius said, Christ was not equal to God. Stern opposition to that was led by a deacon named Athanasius, who had accompanied his bishop to the Council and would himself become the bishop of Alexandria three years later. The Council finally ruled against Arius, but not until the debate became so heated that Arius was reportedly punched in the face.

The Council of Nicaea didn't resolve everything, and it didn't put an end to all competing beliefs and movements, as is made clear by the diversity within Christianity in our own time. However, the fact that the Council was called by a Roman emperor, who himself attended, gave it an authority that it might not otherwise have had. Out of it came the framework of the Nicene Creed, the first uniform statement of Christian doctrine as it is commonly accepted today. The Council devoted so much effort to the angry debate between Arius and Athanasius about the nature of Christ that its initial creed made only a brief mention of the Holy Ghost (or Holy Spirit). However, that was corrected as part of an extended ending of the creed added in 381 CE by a council in Constantinople, giving us the Nicene Creed as we have it today.

Although it originated in the territory of the Eastern church (Constantine's capital was Constantinople, the old Byzantium and present-day Istanbul), the Nicene Creed is accepted today not just by the Eastern Orthodox Church but by many Western churches, such as Roman Catholicism and many Protestant sects.

At the same time, another creed was developing in the West, the Apostles' Creed, so named not because it was written in its present form by any apostles but because it was thought to reflect the beliefs of the apostles. There is much more uncertainty about the development of the Apostles' Creed than the Nicene Creed, since historical records show no church leaders or council that took the lead in writing the creed as a whole.

The Apostles' Creed likely has roots earlier than the Nicene Creed, since it seems to come from a time when there was less emphasis on the detailed nature of Christ and the Holy Spirit. It may have begun to develop as early as the second century as a Roman baptismal statement of faith about the Father, Son, and Holy Spirit, following the formula in Matt 28:19 about baptizing in their name. The writings of some early church fathers reflect some portions of the creed, but the earliest known written record of the complete creed largely as we know it is from the eighth century

Eastern Orthodox churches do not use the Apostles' Creed in their liturgies, but many churches of the West do. A common adaptation of the creed is to present its sections in question form for acknowledgement as part of the liturgy for baptism, fittingly going back to what was perhaps the creed's first use.

The creeds lead us toward the final pieces to solve the mystery of Christianity's origins as identified in the first chapter of this book. Both creeds have evolved into versions with slight differences over the years, in part as some churches have adapted them to meet their own theological requirements. For example, in keeping with its beliefs the Eastern Orthodox Church uses a version of the Nicene Creed that says the Holy Spirit proceeds solely from the Father, rather than from both the Father and the Son. Here is a traditional version of the Nicene Creed, followed by a traditional version of the Apostles' Creed:

The Nicene Creed

I believe in one God:
the Father Almighty,
maker of heaven and earth,
and of all things visible and invisible;

And in one Lord Jesus Christ,
the only begotten Son of God:
begotten of his Father before all worlds,
God of God, Light of Light,
very God of very God,
begotten, not made,
being of one substance with the Father,
through whom all things were made;
who for us men and for our salvation came down from heaven,
and was incarnate by the Holy Ghost of the Virgin Mary, and
was made man;
and was crucified also for us under Pontius Pilate;
he suffered and was buried,
and the third day he rose again according to the Scriptures,
and ascended into heaven,
and sitteth on the right hand of the Father;
and he shall come again, with glory, to judge both the quick
and the dead;
whose kingdom shall have no end.

And I believe in the Holy Ghost, the Lord, the giver of life,
who proceedeth from the Father and the Son;
who with the Father and the Son together is worshiped and
glorified,
who spake by the Prophets.

And I believe in one holy catholic and apostolic Church.
I acknowledge one baptism for the remission of sins.
And I look for the resurrection of the dead, and the life of the
world to come. Amen.[6]

The Apostles' Creed

I believe in God, the Father Almighty, maker of heaven and
earth;

And in Jesus Christ, his only Son, our Lord:
who was conceived by the Holy Spirit,
born of the virgin Mary,
suffered under Pontius Pilate,
was crucified, dead, and buried;
the third day he rose from the dead;
he ascended into heaven,
and sitteth at the right hand of God the Father Almighty;
from thence he shall come to judge the quick and the dead.

I believe in the Holy Spirit,
the holy catholic church,
the communion of saints,
the forgiveness of sins,
the resurrection of the body,
and the life everlasting. Amen.[7]

Notice that both of these creeds follow the same pattern of three
sections: first God, then Jesus Christ, and then the Holy Ghost (or
Holy Spirit). Thus, saying them is a reminder of the doctrine of the
Trinity.

Both creeds use the word "catholic" in referring to the church.
Catholics generally capitalize it and see it as referring to their
church. Protestants usually don't capitalize it and see it as referring
in general to the church universal.

Neither the Nicene Creed nor the Apostles' Creed gives a detailed theory of atonement, but there have been many theories. One
of the earliest is the ransom theory, saying that the death of Jesus was
a ransom paid to Satan. There is the moral example theory, saying
that the death of Jesus was to set an inspiring example to encourage

repentance and right action by others. Those two examples are certainly not a complete list of early views, but they bring us to the most commonly held view today, the penal satisfaction theory. It states that Jesus died a substitutionary death to satisfy a God of justice by taking upon himself the penalty deserved by others.

The one thing that all traditional views of atonement have in common is that the death of Jesus was necessary. Even in its vagueness about how atonement works, the Nicene Creed plays a critical role in establishing as orthodoxy the belief that the death of Jesus was essential. It makes that especially clear by saying that Jesus "for our salvation came down from heaven" and "was crucified also for us."

The Nicene Creed also mentions "one baptism for the remission of sins." In this, a traditional understanding has been that in baptism forgiveness of sins comes by participating through grace in the benefits of the sacrificial act of Christ. Today the various branches within Christendom differ substantially in their understanding of baptism. One issue is that of infant baptism versus the baptism only of persons old enough to make their own faith commitment. Also, some Christians believe baptism is necessary for salvation and others believe it is not, and some such as the Quakers do not practice it at all.

The much shorter Apostles' Creed does not specifically say that the death of Jesus was for the purpose of making salvation possible. However, many Christians assume this is understood by its mention of the suffering of Jesus and the forgiveness of sins.

One thing both creeds have in common is that they proclaim a religion *about* Jesus at the cost of ignoring the religion *of* Jesus. Both the Nicene and Apostles' Creeds leap directly from the birth of Jesus to his death. As a result, someone who knows Christianity only from those creeds can have no idea of the broad scope of Jesus' teachings.

Finally, it is especially important to remember that through the positions they take the creeds are not just affirmations of faith but denials of any contradictory views. The creeds were written as much to reject some beliefs as to affirm others. Their wide acceptance means that today most Christians are unaware of the fact that other views were once contenders for what the most widely accepted Christian doctrine should be.

We can easily imagine how early church leaders—who were Gentiles and never recited the Jewish confession of faith proclaiming the oneness of God, the Shema—might have found no problem with seeing Jesus as a deity. It is more difficult to understand why they rejected a God of such great mercy that he requires only sincere repentance and reconciliation with others, in favor of a God who required that Jesus be tortured to death. We will look more deeply at this issue in the next chapter, but statements by Jesus in the first three gospels make clear that seeing him as a deity and as a sacrifice would have highly offended him. Unfortunately, the full details of the discussions critical to how Christianity evolved centuries ago are lost to history. But the results include the list of New Testament books that we now have and the Nicene and Apostles' Creeds that Christians have recited ever since.

11

What This Means for Today

After the destruction of the Temple in 70 CE there were only two Jewish sects remaining, the Pharisees and the Jesus sect. Most Jews chose the Pharisees because the Jesus sect offered them nothing they needed. Jesus had not turned out to be their sought-after messiah. That is, he did not gather the nations, throw out the Romans, and set up a new kingdom of righteousness on earth. And they did not need Jesus to set right their relationship with God. Temple sacrifice was now impossible without the Temple. But, as we have seen, even before the fall of the Temple there was a strong movement toward understanding God to be so merciful that he requires not the shedding of blood but only a truly contrite heart. And most importantly, as it would have been viewed by any Jew including Jesus himself, seeing a person as divine violated the most basic tenet of their monotheistic faith.

There is a sad twist here. Christianity has traditionally been presented by its adherents as the one and only path to salvation, made possible by the sacrificial death of Jesus. Tragically that has often led to a brutal arrogance that is so misguided it turns upside down what Jesus said about the necessity for people to first offer grace to one another. As we have seen, Jesus had the highest scorn for blood sacrifice, saying that instead God seeks sincere repentance and especially a willingness to forgive others. In large part, what angered some powerful people enough to demand the execution of Jesus was the uncompromising stand he took against sacrifices that were very profitable to them. Jesus felt so strongly about this that if he were to walk into a modern-day service of the Eucharist, depicting not only his body as an offering for sin but even the drinking of his blood, it is easy to imagine another angry cleansing of the Temple.

This leads us to a startling fact: because of a tradition that began even before Jesus, it has long been Judaism with its emphasis on repentance that has best been in step with his teachings on how to reconcile with God. Meanwhile, Christianity has dismissed the

87

teachings of Jesus on this and symbolically gone back to the bloody days of the Temple with Jesus himself as the sacrifice. Owing to Jewish dissent on that and other points, Christianity became a religion primarily of Gentiles who had no previous traditions about means of salvation or reciting the Shema.

There is obvious irony in this, not just for Christianity but for Judaism as well. Jesus put his life on the line by challenging Temple sacrifice and proclaiming a God of mercy who requires only a contrite heart. But when the destruction of the Temple in 70 CE made impossible the sacrificial practices that Jesus had opposed, Judaism survived the loss by embracing the same tradition of repentance that Jesus had followed. It underlies the understanding of the High Holy Days and the most sacred day in the Jewish calendar, Yom Kippur, the Day of Atonement.

This leaves us with an important question that takes us back to the Aaronite priests who, as we saw in Chapter 3, sought centuries before the birth of Jesus to consolidate their authority and increase their income by introducing the idea that God's forgiveness comes through blood sacrifice. Many people of Old Testament times rejected that, Jesus and many other Jews of his time rejected it, and Jews of today reject it—all in favor of viewing God as far too merciful to require such a thing. The only ones yet remaining under the spell of those Aaronite priests are Christians. And they have typically been oblivious to the fact that their belief in the need for a Lamb of God ultimately has its source in a self-serving and disputed effort by some priests to increase their power and wealth more than two and half thousand years ago.

The question this presents is this: With a much less brutal option clearly open to them, why did the early Christian leaders who gave us our creeds choose the God of strict justice who can't forgive without the shedding of blood? The answer may come down to a simple fact: If God forgives through repentance and there is no need for blood sacrifice, the cross may be viewed as a symbol of failure in Jesus' promise to bring in a new age of righteousness on earth within the lifetime of some then living. The messianic age on earth never came, and Christians—especially church leaders whose prestige and livelihood have depended on promoting Christianity—are even today loath to say that Jesus failed at anything.

It can even be argued that seeing Jesus as an offering for sin is what allowed Christianity to thrive as a religion, and that without it Christianity may not have obtained a wide enough following to still exist today. It is not particularly motivating to say Jesus was a man who taught that salvation comes from a merciful God simply through repentance, and who was executed for angering the Temple authorities on that point and annoying the Romans by trying to bring in the messianic age. It is much easier to make converts by saying that Jesus is God who came to earth to die for your sins, and by threatening wrath to come if you don't believe that. Filling people with the fear of hellfire and then offering a remedy as simple as just believing something was so effective that what Jesus actually taught couldn't compete.

The support by Emperor Constantine of a state-approved church finally assured the defeat of all early opposing views, including those of Jesus himself and the disciples who walked with him. There was a time when traditional Christian doctrine need not have become what it is today, but early church leaders made the choices that they felt would most benefit them. As a result, in a kind of religious Darwinism, Christianity evolved more to fulfill an agenda of creating converts to enhance the status and fortunes of the church than to respect the teachings of the man for whom it is named.

For Christians today, the understanding of Jesus as a blood sacrifice is reinforced through creeds and rituals such as the observance of the Lord's Supper. But that still does not explain why Christians can hear in church a gospel passage about John the Baptist offering a baptism of repentance for the forgiveness of sins and then not question a sermon a few minutes later that says that salvation comes only through the sacrificial death of Jesus. And it does not explain how pastors can lead their congregations in the words of the Lord's Prayer asking God to forgive them as they forgive others and then deliver a sermon that says that God's forgiveness is possible only through the torturous death of Jesus on the cross. As noted in Chapter 2, some people become so set on what they want to believe that reading anything different in the Bible simply makes no impression at all.

At this point something should probably be said about the hope of a Second Coming, and especially about the book of Revelation.

That book was not admitted into the New Testament canon until the end of the fourth century, and then only after long and contentious debate. One argument against it was that it was so strange and difficult that it would lead to highly fanciful interpretations. It is an understatement to say that prediction has been borne out. Perhaps more significantly, everyone who has ever predicted an imminent end of the age has turned out to be wrong. Taking Jesus seriously means acknowledging that even he was mistaken on that matter. If even he could not do it, how can anyone else be so presumptuous as to think they can?

Although in its liturgy Christianity still looks toward the return of Christ, in actual practice many churches have long acted as if, with regard to a visible earthly presence, we have seen the last of Jesus. In other words, they have concluded that if his ministry is to continue it must be through them.

This raises the issue of what relevance there can be today to a religion built on the conflicting foundations of Christianity. Jesus was clearly not a Christian, not just because that term did not yet exist in his lifetime but also because he would have abhorred the most fundamental tenets of Christianity. For it is a religion that rejects the beliefs about reconciliation with God and neighbor that Jesus strongly held, in favor of a theory of blood sacrifice that he totally opposed. And in worshipping Jesus as a deity Christianity applies to him the same pagan principle that was behind the imperial cults of Rome, in heinous violation of what Jesus said was the most important commandment of his faith. On those two points alone the church has ignored the Jesus of history to create a religion that he would have firmly rejected.

It is as if Christian leaders decided long ago, and still insist, that Jesus of Nazareth cannot be allowed to contradict the Christ of the church's creation. But the problems underlying Christianity run much deeper. It claims to be a religion based on the reality of certain events, but those events include a virgin birth told in two stories that are hugely in conflict with both one another and the known history of that time, and which are refuted even by the words of the Apostle Paul. It declares as the messiah a man who failed to meet the messianic expectations of his time. It believes in a resurrection that would have been foremost an opportunity for Jesus to dramatically proclaim a special status with an appearance before the very people who condemned and crucified him. That such a thing never happened suggests that it was not possible. Finally, because of rejection by most Jews for reasons Jesus himself would have understood, Christianity has become largely a religion only of Gentiles, in spite of the fact that in conducting his ministry Jesus said he intended to offer them nothing.

As for what might be the most reasonable response in our own time, some simply find religion irrelevant to their lives or even actively reject it as man-made. Atheists in particular see Christianity's historical, biblical, and logical discrepancies as among their reasons to reject altogether any belief in God. For many, revealing Christianity as a fabricated faith that ignores even teachings of Jesus leads to the conclusion that even a faith based more fully on what Jesus taught would also be just another human invention.

Another option is to continue with traditional faith, ignoring anything that does not fit one's preconceptions. People who do this commonly insist that they have a great and unshakable faith, often coupled with angry intolerance for those who do not believe as they do. However, for some of them a highly heated defensiveness suggests a great unease.

Finally, some may be drawn to a spiritual quest outside of traditional Christianity, including as one of many options the choice of finding a greater respect for the actual Jesus of Nazareth and his teachings without worshiping him. And in that those who continue to believe in a power beyond themselves may come to see the true good news of the gospel as being even better than commonly portrayed. For in Jesus they can see a man who proclaimed a God of such great love and mercy that the need for any redemptive shedding of blood is unthinkable, and who especially called people to offer and seek reconciliation with one another. Combined with the importance that Jesus placed on outreach to those who are needy in body and spirit, his may be seen as a message that transcends time and space and even any specific religion.

Notes

1. Richard Elliott Friedman, *Who Wrote the Bible?*, 2nd ed. (New York: HarperCollins, 1997). Readers who wish to know more about how the Torah, the first five books of the Bible, developed can find a very readable and detailed presentation in Friedman's book.
2. See Friedman, *Who Wrote the Bible?* 87–88.
3. See additional discussion of this theme in Friedman, *Who Wrote the Bible?* 144–45, 238–41.
4. All quotations from 1 Enoch are from R. H. Charles, *The Book of Enoch* (London: Society for Promoting Christian Knowledge, 1917).
5. *Gates of Prayer* (New York: Central Conference of American Rabbis, 1975), 393.
6. The version of the Nicene Creed in this book is from *The Methodist Hymnal* (Nashville: The Methodist Publishing House, 1964).
7. The version of the Apostles' Creed in this book is the traditional version from *The United Methodist Hymnal* (Nashville: The United Methodist Publishing House, 1989).

Index

About the Author

Richard Hagenston is an ordained United Methodist minister and former pastor. He holds a Master of Divinity degree from Wesley Theological Seminary and a master's in journalism from Indiana University.

CPSIA information can be obtained at www.ICGtesting.com
Printed in the USA
LVOW04s0015020914

401964LV00013B/412/P